HOW I *Let* HER STEAL MY HUSBAND

BY

NADIA MATHEWS

FOREWARD

The shear courage and unadulterated selflessness that has been captured through the carefully articulated words on the pages of this book must be applauded. Without regard for how others may view her, Nadia Mathews has allowed her life story to be exposed so that following generations can bypass similar mistakes that she herself had to live. This story is captivating and heart-wrenching, compelling and awe-striking. I found myself having to hold back tears as her words ministered to me and her experiences reached inside of me and found something to connect to. As an author, she has done what very few are truly willing to do. She has exposed her wounds in order to heal the hearts of others and mend the spirits of the broken. It is my prayer that millions are able to partake of the feast of knowledge, wisdom and truth that I have been privileged to consume.

I met Nadia some years ago as she spoke the words to me that I have heard time and time again, "Oh you write, me too." Little did I know that she had a story to tell. Many people live every day and experience life's many pitfalls, disappointments and fiascos. They then go on to make their best effort to pray away the situations and somehow forget the pain, but a chosen few are willing to share their story. A chosen few are willing to dig deep and claw at wounds that have been closed and allow the tears to re-emerge and the pain to be relived all so that they can help someone else who may be hurting.

This is not just a book, it's a testimony. The Word of God says, "They triumphed over him by the blood of the Lamb and by the Word of their testimony," *Revelations 12:11,* New International Version. The only way to truly triumph is by embracing what happened and using it to fight with. Let this testimony be a war cry that we will no longer stand for mediocrity, but we will pursue excellence in our lives and in our relationships. Take heed to the warnings catalogued in this book and embrace the knowledge that it contains. She speaks with wisdom beyond her years because she had to live the ordeals that I pray not even my worst enemy would have to endure. Marriage is a beautiful thing and divorce is perhaps the ugliest, most hurtful and harming tool I've seen the enemy use. I beg every individual, both men and women to read this book and allow it to minister, encourage and enlighten you because it can happen to you. No matter how saved you are, how sanctified you are or how incredibly filled with the Holy Ghost you might be, if you let it, life will happen and you will find yourself looking up wondering "How did I get here and how do I get out?" I give much kudos to Nadia and this grand piece of art. If we displayed stories like we do pictures, this one could hang next to the Mona Lisa and be right at home. This book will set the captives free and help individuals to realize that there is life after loss and dead things can live again if we let go AND let God have His way.

God Bless,

Pastor R. Shamar Walker

DEDICATION

This book is dedicated first to Christ the one true love in my life. It continues to my beautiful daughters Laila Grace, Kayla Marie and Audrey Rose. You have been a lifeline to mommy when I flat lined. I am also eternally grateful to Lee my wonderful patient king that has held me under the worst of times and laughed with me during the fun times. You are one of God's greatest gifts to me and I couldn't have asked for a better man if I drew you with my own pen. You have helped me find that all the strength I will ever need resides inside of me. Thank you Bishop Vinson for teaching me that being true to myself is the only way to be delivered. To my Pastor and First Lady Jasson and Keisha Randolph you have fed me a Word that has blessed my soul and I am so blessed to call my First lady and mentor also my friend. Lady Randolph, in the 15 years that we have been best friends, I've grown tremendously as a woman. You have always been there no matter what to counsel and encourage me. I am blessed and grateful that God gave me you. To my Parents that have put up with me, supported me, and took care of my daughters with the same love you gave me. Thank you and just remember Mommy that you had to feel those birth pains! To my Dawnee you are the epitome of a real woman and I take many cues from you.... To my girls Jew-Jew, Momo and Lona y'all have cried with me, prayed with me and had to listen to when I thought a line was better than another. I love you chicks! To everyone that spoke life into me I am blessed because you love me!

All my love,

Nadia Mathews

HOW I LET HER STEAL MY HUSBAND
BY
NADIA MATHEWS

How did I let her steal my husband???

One year later as I sit in front of a blank sheet of paper, tears welling in my eyes and only my memories to keep me warm, I ask myself this very question, how did I let her steal my husband? There is a tormenting voice echoing in my head replaying the five years of our broken marriage. I tell God that I will never let another woman of God make the mistakes I did. I'll tell you my story line for line, memory for memory and open my scars, but only if you promise to listen. Only if you promise to take a long look at your own view of marriage and everything that happens before, during and after. The lines that follow are easier for you to read than they were for me to write, but I pray that this helps you.

My First Mistake Was... 1

My story begins 2,190 days ago when life seemed to be perfect and the only thing I thought I was missing was a man. At the age of 19, my definition of a man was a 6 foot 4 inch, 200 pound, deep dark complexion with a killer smile and a car, nothing more, nothing less. My list of wants were more than needs and completely vain. The best way to illustrate the beginning of what I thought was my "happy ending," is to tell you my journey into womanhood, marriage, motherhood and mayhem.

I am still in my twenties and I have lived through losing a child, losing my morals, losing my standards and living through divorce. Now I'm sure you're wondering when the juicy stuff is coming, but know that whatever your reason was to get this book, I pray that after you read this the way you view love, life and relationships is forever changed. I warn you however, if you're looking for me to point a finger and condemn anyone I'm afraid you sadly made the wrong decision to read this book. I won't paint a pretty picture of myself but rather the opposite. Some may even think I've gone too far, but I know that so much of my growth as a mother and person has come from being able to define and identify my mistakes and not allow those mistakes to define me.

Before we jump in, I want to quickly say a quick prayer:

"Dear Heavenly Father I want to first come to you and thank you for the person that picked up this book. Father because they sowed into me, Father I pray that you send it back to them double because of their sacrifice. Lord, I pray that every word written touches them in a place that brings repentance for some and healing in others. I pray that God, you are glorified and in my words they feel your grace. I thank you in advance for allowing me to be used and others blessed. In Jesus name... Amen"

Let's start at my favorite part, the beginning..... I was a skinny 19 year old girl with not much to offer anyone but my passion for young people and my sternness against the Word "NO." My father, still to this day, refers to me as "Rock." He's always said that if you tell Nadia "NO" you can bet that she'll still find a way to do it. I guess that's a very accurate statement because over the years I hit my head on that Rock so many times I felt like I was dying inside. I grew up while attending Greater Fellowship Baptist Church. As I went home every day I noticed this building up the street from my house that changed residents very closely to how often I changed my view of the world. It started as a super market then turned into to a specialty shop and finally became a church. I would say to myself often, "I guess they are going to try their hand in Jesus since nothing ever seemed to work." One day I came home from work and heard my parents arguing. The arguments were often pertaining to me. My parents hadn't heard me arrive home, and I heard a conversation that no one should hear coming from their parents. I would love to say that my childhood was a bed of roses and that I was angelic, but that was not the case. As any other teenager, I thought I knew everything and challenged my parents at any opportunity. Becoming upset, I ran from the house as tears ran down my face. I walked up the street feeling as lonely as I had ever been in my life. The truth was that I was adopted when I was three years old. It's one thing to be unruly and be genetically linked to your parents, but when you're not even in the gene pool, then you feel worse about not being the "chosen one." Growing up I never felt like I belonged, but it wasn't because my parents didn't include me, it was simply because I knew I didn't. I longed to know the woman that birthed and carried me. Sadly before God allowed my birth cousin to walk into Pizza Hut and accidentally introduce herself; my birth mother had passed away. All I knew about my mother was that she was addicted to drugs and had been promiscuous. Those are indubitably the two facts no girl wants to know about the legacy of her past. I fought so hard not to become as my mother often said "the apple that didn't fall to far from the tree." I was willing to do anything that could possibly promise to give another life free from that type of reality. Anyone else's definition of me was better than the definition that my family thought I was doomed to repeat. So as I walked up the street that day, I noticed that the church I had seen many days was opened and in I went. I sat in the back and listened to a young man speak about how important it was to be prepared for y2k and how he could supply some instrument that would hold essentials necessary for survival to help make the transition smoother for each family. I thought to myself, "So you're contemplating suicide and you decided to come into a church that's having a meeting, great choice Nadia." I sat in the back and I noticed a good friend from High School there. Seeing me upset, he came over and offered me prayer. We went into a different room and a few people came in and told me that after prayer I should be filled with the Holy Ghost. They explained this would make me talk funny but it was the spirit of God speaking through me concerning my needs. I was lost and not receptive to this new teaching, but I welcomed the prayer. After their well wishes, I returned home. That was the beginning of the moments destined to change my life forever.

I went home and after the house settled, I waited a few weeks and told my parents that I would be going to a new church. They told me that was a choice of mine, but if I lived with them that I had to go to their church. I disagreed and I moved out for the first time. I joined that new church and it was the best decision I ever made.

Before beginning college, I joined a new church called Temple of Praise. It was full of spirit-filled praying men and women of God. Under the leadership of Bishop R.L. Vinson and Pastor Linda Vinson, this ministry had showed me that worshipping God didn't have to be about boundaries and tradition. Worshiping God was free flowing and full of life. Bishop Vinson challenged my views on religion and taught me that without a relationship with God it would be impossible to live Holy. During that time I felt the Lord leading me in the direction of young people, so I was eager to begin learning how to help other young people learn what the Lord was teaching me. As I began my walk with God, I met a young man named Mike that instantly captured my heart. Our relationship grew fast. My love for our expanding youth department grew equally as fast. Every month in our youth service we had an open forum. During this forum many youth were speaking candidly about their concerns and things that were hindering their walk with God. One of the more popular youth leaders took the stage and began to encourage the young people. Before giving up the microphone, he began to describe the hardships of being single and describing how God was going to send him a pure virgin wife that only knew him. She would be someone that stood behind him and encouraged him as he was growing in God. Accompanying me to this event was my louder best friend Keisha. She nudged me during his speech and rolled her eyes.

"Who does this guy think he is," she whispered.

"I know, right?" I agreed, secretly wanting to hear more from this apparently popular leader.

"Well I'm going to call him out."

Before anyone could stop her, she was already up and walking toward the microphone. I knew as soon as she had a platform, she would give this man a piece of her thoughts and she dare him to rebut her. She was as powerful and captivating with a microphone then as she is now. Walking confidently to the podium she grabbed the microphone, defiantly looking in his direction, she asked:

"Are you a virgin?" Her tone was intimidating and dominant. The time between her interrogation and his answer felt like an eternity. The moment he opened his mouth we all knew the answer that would follow.

"No." He looked embarrassed and caught off guard but I imagine intrigued by the 100 pound, bold, dynamo with the audacity to question him at his event.

Looking incredibly embarrassed and caught off guard, he shook his head and quietly said "No."

Ready, aim, fire, was the attitude Keisha took toward the arrogant leader "How can you condemn a woman who may have fallen into fornication before you and you're not even a virgin? A woman shouldn't be defined by her mistakes but by the way she changes them."

The crowd all hushed waiting for the leader to respond but sadly he did not. She placed her weapon, the microphone, back in its stand and sashayed to her seat next to me.

"I can't believe you said that Keisha," I chuckled.

I had known Keisha since the seventh grade. Watching her boldness gave me the courage to speak up against things in which I didn't believe. I always knew she was stronger than me, but I hadn't considered how strong I was until much later in my life.

"Well I can't believe he said that to the youth," she whispered.

Shortly after his admission the nameless leader decided to end the forum. The leader gave the benediction and the young people rose. Everyone scattered and conversations were buzzing around us. Mini-crowds of people around the church were chattering about school and random church teenage gossip.

After the forum, as the youth were leaving, I decided I wanted to meet this man. As I was approaching him I thought of how I would strike up a conversation. I watched in amazement at how the youth responded to the leader. They rallied around him like he was the president of some exclusive club that they wanted to be included. He hugged the boys, pretended to shadow box with some and gave others affectionate "nougats." I was intrigued by his charm and all I knew was that I too wanted to be a part of this exclusive club and learn how to affect young people the way he did. I approached him while he was talking to some of the youth and he stopped

"Hi, I enjoyed the forum today," I said.

"Thanks, I'm sorry I don't think we've met my name is David. Where's your friend?" David asked looking around me for my friend, the loud one that challenged him.

"Oh, Keisha, she's conversing with some mutual friends of ours. I'm Nadia. I guess she caught you off guard?"

"No not really. Why didn't you come to the youth function at my house this past weekend?"

"How old do you think I am, David?" I asked laughing at his assumption that I was the age of the teens he was just playing with.

"I'm sorry I hope I didn't offend you. You look really young. How old are you?"

As I was about to answer, Keisha arrived on the scene. There were introductions and the conversation shifted to their previous conversation about his fantasy bride. I just stood by and watched the two engage in banter. I'm sure he was eager to meet the woman that caused him a slight embarrassment and the woman that sniggled at his response to the spotlight. While David was defending his view, I watched his lips turn from the slight scowl to reveal the greatest smile I had ever seen. He began to tell us how long he had been working with the youth department and I assumed that he must have been feeling partially inadequate as he went to defend himself against Keisha's words but they went unheard because she only tuned in enough to find enough evidence to disprove his theory, whatever it was! That was the beginning of their friendship and being her best friend meant my involvement in as much.

My love for the youth was growing and my relationship with God was changing. My view on life was different and my desire for the Word of God was also growing. Sadly my relationship with Mike was unraveling. After some trouble at home, Mike's parents had taken me in and we were fighting every day. I had turned to David a few times for counsel. I remember being in prayer circle and David giving me a prophetic word that God would bring me back to Atlanta sooner than I thought from college. He also said God would heal me from my break up with Mike. He was always preaching to me about how God wouldn't bless our union if we had broken the instructions of God. As long as Mike and I were in sin in any way, God would never allow us to stay together. David was slowly becoming my friend always there to listen, to pray and give me Godly wisdom. I admired him when he told me how he was planning a trip to North Carolina to witness and Keisha and I should come along. I jumped at another chance to learn from him.

The trip was spontaneous and unplanned. A welcomed distraction from the strife between Mike and I. Keisha, David, another close friend Jamal and I set off on a journey to tell people about Jesus. The long ride gave us plenty of time to talk and get to know each other. I found David funny and witty.

"So how did you meet Mike?" David asked

"Well we met after church one day. He's a nice guy but we're having a few setbacks," I told David reluctantly.

I wanted as much time away from the drama that surrounded my relationship as possible.

"Well I'm not trying to be nosey. We can just talk about something else," David said. I guess he could sense that the conversation would make me feel uncomfortable. We had done a good job thus far just keeping the conversation about Jesus. Ministry and Youth counseling was all we ever talked about. I rattled on about my family and the stories about my life. I found it easy to talk to him about life and he was always very attentive and engaging.

We arrived in North Carolina late that evening and prayed for two people that received Christ. David and I took a few minutes alone and walked along the beach sharing stories about how we came to Christ. Our journeys were so different, but our need to affect the world drew us together. Somewhere along the beach, I began to look at him as more than just a friend in Christ. We stole away for a little while. After I changed into my bathing suit, he threw me in the water and we laughed. For the first time in months, I was having fun.

On the ride home, I realized that the most rewarding part of this trip was watching the souls that came to Christ. We prayed for them as David had baptized them. The will of God and drawing souls to Christ was a beautiful thing. I was so glad to be a part of it. Even though our trip was beautiful, returning home to a broken relationship was hard. Mike and I were over and no matter how heart broken I was I couldn't stop thinking about much fun it was embracing God's people and learning about the ways of God during our private Bible study. The Bible study had become the highlight of my week. It was the opportunity to learn everything from paying tithes to soul winning. The hardest transition would be going to college after the summer of revelations and making new friendships because I knew the fun was coming to an end.

The day before I left, I was laying across my bed thinking about my future when my phone rang.

"Hey Nadia, its David. What time are you leaving in the morning?" David said. I could hear there was a lot of noise in the background.

"Around eight-ish I think. What is all that noise over there?"

"I'm at a friend's house playing cards. I just wanted to say good luck and I'll talk to you when you get back."

I was happy that he had called but I could tell there was something else he wanted to say.

"If you're not busy maybe you should come by and see me off," I stuttered out. It seemed like a long time before he answered.

"No, I can't we just started the game and it's kind of late," David said.

I looked at the clock on the wall that read 8:30 p.m. and I guessed that he was probably right. Disappointed, I said, "Ok well e-mail me when you get some time."

"I will. Be good down there at Albany State and make sure you study your Word. Talk to you later."

Looking at the phone, feeling rejected, I placed it back on the cradle and laid down. I did what any other young woman does after feeling dejected by her crush, I called my best friend to, of course, reaffirm how wonderful I really was. As I described to her what seemed to be one of the most horrific things that ever happened to me (I was defiantly melodramatic) call waiting clicked in interrupting my explanation. Annoyed, I transferred lines to hear:

"Hey, I think I will come see you off before you leave," it was David's voice.

"Cool, can you pick up Keisha before you come by? I want to say goodbye to her too?"

"Yeah, we'll see you in a little while," he replied.

I hid that the real reason that I had never been alone with David was that I was uncomfortable about what to say to him after it was obvious that I liked it a little more than I should. I had only held Christian conversations with him and I was certain that his visit meant more than just seeing off a good Christian sister to college, at least I hoped it was. Our conversation since the soul saving venture had been limited because I was getting over my relationship with Mike. I remember the anticipation and butterflies I had a strange feeling in my tummy waiting for David and Keisha to arrive. I remember looking out the window and pacing back and forth in my room before I saw his headlights shining in my window. He parked at the top of the hill and I ran downstairs. Gathering myself from my sprint, which seemed like I was running 100 yards to the door, I took one last look in the mirror that hung next to our front door and turned the knob.

I raced up the hill the same way I did when I met my biological sisters a year before. I swung open the door and sat down in the back seat of his car. His crush velvet seats felt familiar and soft against my leg. Keisha was the first to say hello. For the next 30 minutes, we laughed as they gave me advice on school and bid me farewell. As we talked, I occasionally found myself wanting to touch him, not in a sexual way but just to be closer to him. It's crazy. His smile was like nothing that I had ever seen. I believe that was the day that I fell in love, or at least what I thought was love. He told me that he would come and see me sometimes at school. I said that would be great and before I knew it our moment was over, we hugged and he was gone.

It's crazy that I don't remember what we talked about in great detail, but I can describe how I felt around him. I was ready to take on college because back home I had a great guy friend praying and interceding for me. He did exactly as he said and I saw him when I came home one weekend a few short weeks later.

One day during one of my many visits home, David had invited me over. We went walking in a park holding hands. He began to tell me about how he acquired his home and how shortly after that he brought his mother and sister to Covington from Florida to live with him. I admired him more watching the care he took of his mother and sister with little thought of his personal life. He described how he had been celibate, saving himself for that woman of God that he would marry. He had been married before and unfortunately it had been unsuccessful. Since then he had found it was time to focus on the people of God, especially the young people. He wouldn't make that mistake again. He was like the pages of great novel unfolding before me. I just couldn't get enough of his honesty. As we approached the house hand in hand, the silence in the air created a nervous energy that I hadn't felt in my life before. Opening the door, we retreated to his bedroom to talk. I was unsure of where to sit, so I just propped on the wall closest to the door. Glancing around the small space, I noticed his room was plain and undecorated.

His room had a full size bed with some Aztec multi colored print on the sheets. His wall was white washed with nothing hanging on them. He had a small TV on a microwave cart that looked like something that he must have picked up from the thrift store because it had the digital gauge on the dial and he didn't have a remote. I looked around and thought, wow, my dorm room looks more put together than this.

"David who's idea was it to put this pattern in your room?" I asked. Almost laughing at the choice of colors in an adult's room, I asked.

"My Grandmother made these sheets for me and well I just put them on the bed. I don't know anything about all this decorating stuff," David said, looking around like maybe he should have been offended, but not knowing quite what to say about his simple tastes. I looked across the hall at the much bigger suite that his mother occupied. I couldn't help but smile at his visible generosity towards his mother. He was very attentive and protective of his mother and his little sister, as they were of him. The room was similar in simplicity but much bigger then it seemed and the bed had bricks underneath to provide more height to the bed. I found out that this was an old country trick to make the bed sit higher off the ground.

We laughed. At some point during the next few minutes I got up off the floor and sat on the bed beside him. Wanting to be closer, I laid down on my back staring at the ceiling. We were both watching it like it was playing some new sci-fi flick that we had been dying to see. The conversation was merely a distraction from the passion that was simmering underneath our words. All I wanted to do was kiss him. I wanted to tell him to hush, that I didn't want to talk about school and church. I wanted to know that he looked at me like a man looks at a woman and not just be my church mentor.

"Oh…," I said hoping that he was too was feeling the energy in the air. I was stuttering for something to say feeling slightly embarrassed for insulting his homemade linens. I was so nervous that I began to ramble about school.

"The prayer group has been going well. I have been going to some services down there and..." I just began to muddle on and right in the middle of a pretty awkward moment, he rolled over and kissed me. It wasn't that awkward first time kiss, but one filled with longing and passion. The longer we kissed, the more evident it became that if God didn't intervene, we were in the danger zone– not of losing clothes– but in losing our hearts. I knew that kiss would be the first of many. I can still feel the ripple of his heart beating against the fabric of my t-shirt that day. I just knew this was what they talked about in movies, the feeling that song writers can't stop writing about. I was falling for this Religious type of guy and I couldn't be saved. Just when the moment began to get intense, his little sister swung open the door waking us from our trance. I sprang up from the bed and adjusting my disheveled clothes, I hoped that Alecia hadn't witnessed our moment. As I looked up from my embarrassment, his brown eyes met mine. I lingered there in his eyes for a second and dashed from the room. Walking up the hall toward the great smells in the kitchen, I had the widest grin on my face.

Mama Karen was cooking her famous jerk chicken with and rice and peas and I joined in to watch. We chatted about nothing in particular while I watched her cook her famous meal. After dinner David retreated back to his room leaving his mother and I again alone to talk.

"You know Nadia I want my son to have a wife like you that will clean up and take care of him," she said.

I was startled by her candor about her son's romantic life. I guess she must have heard my heart skipping a beat during dinner looking over at David. Sheepishly, I looked at her stopped, moving the broom and said, "Oh Ms. Mom, David and I aren't dating."

It wasn't like you couldn't see what was happening with us. The look she gave me was one of pure sarcasm. I guessed that neither my words nor my actions were convincing enough to prove my statement. That night after our talk, I spent the night in the room with his mother who had just adopted me in as her older daughter. As I lay down, I could see the tiny stream of light peering into our room from David's. I saw him on his knees praying and in my heart I hoped that he prayed the same prayer as I did, "Lord make this real. Don't let me be wrong this time." I was praying that God had made me for him instead of praying for the Will of God. That day, that night, looking into David's eyes changed my life.

My colleges mornings then were filled with e-cards and e-mails from David asking how I was. Every night, I rushed home from a friend's adjoining room to receive his call for prayer. My life seemed perfect. Being in a relationship with David completed it. I was a babe in Christ in love with a man that matched my passion for life and also my love for young people. Destiny had sent us each other. It's amazing how one day your hand seems perfect and before you can catch them, all the cards have slipped from your fingers. We were so heavily flawed but in each other's eyes we were perfect.

We were so young, but what we felt for each other was real and tangible. We embraced each other and gave each other hope for the future we would share helping tomorrows youth to be everything we wished we had become. How cliché and corny it may sound now, but for us it was the only way to solve what we thought was broken in our own youth where we had such different experiences.

NADIA'S STORY

I was the baby girl of three siblings and I struggled most of my life with horrible self-esteem. I was adopted at the age of three and I wondered many times why my biological mother gave me up. I wanted to know what made me the one she let go to the state while my other sisters went with their biological father's family. Yes I had a mother and father now but most of my teenage years I spent fighting with them. I felt like a caged bird under their strict direction and often rebelled verbally because of it. My father was the greatest provider but I can't remember much affection coming from him. I wanted to be beautiful so badly but I never felt that way. I wasn't the popular girl, fiercely skinny, glasses and a birth mark left cheek and a mole in my eye. I can't remember my daddy ever saying I was beautiful until I was much older. I thought that giving my body (to men) made me a woman and that gave me the attention I needed.

ATTENTION FATHERS

Little girls need their daddy. They need you to love them out loud. Tell them every day that they're beautiful. Daddy should be there to support them daily even when they fail and if they don't meet his approval. If you don't, then they will find a father figure and don't be surprised if it's a man your own age. He'll tell her that she is beautiful, worthy, intelligent, and all he's ever wanted. If she were mature for her age any man would be lucky to have her on his arm. She'll smile thinking how lucky she is to have a man's love her for herself. She'll walk differently and smile more from the new found confidence he has given her. That confidence comes at a price because he'll asks her soon to prove to him that she cares for him the way he cares for her. He'll whisper all the right things in her ear while his places his hand down between her legs and bends her over to dishonor her body. She'll cry, but the tears go unheard because he continues with no regard to her tiny body. He'll take her purity. She'll get up from the defiled sheets to wash the shame from her skin, but no matter how many times she scrubs his scent lingers. That night, she'll want to crawl into her father's lap and cry to him about how he hurt her and how she will not go back, but he'll be busy with his own thoughts and won't sense the change in her demeanor. She'll lash out at him now and forever. While she rebels he'll convince himself it is not his fault. He'll tell himself that he's not affectionate and not built for all that lovey-dovey stuff and she just better get over it. All the while his little princess is no longer his princess and has grown up before her time. This is a plea from that little girl crying where no one can hear. That little girl is shamed from her choices. Daddies pay attention, as she needs you. Please don't let her pleas go unanswered. Her life is riding on you as not missing the signs, daddy. Please pay attention daddy before it's too late.

David's Story

David was raised in a single-parent home with limited emotional guidance from his father. Mama Karen wrestled her own personal demons for many years. As time progressed David became the head of the household. He watched his older brother struggle for stability and determined that he would not follow in the same footsteps. He moved from Florida, settled in Atlanta and purchased a home with the support of his extended family. He knew that his mother needed him and brought Mama and Alecia to live with him. I remembered during our marriage I would often tell David that what he felt he was missing in his upbringing from his mother shouldn't keep him from accepting love. He held in his emotions much of his life until he exploded in bouts of rage. If he was challenged, anyone in his path could be subject of those outbursts.

He had one unsuccessful marriage. He was determined to never experience the heartbreak of not just losing a wife but a woman he considered to be a friend.

We were two young people with a lot of pain and heavy baggage coming together looking for a healing in each other when we should have been looking for a healing in the one true God.

> *So often we hear women say they are tired of looking for a man. I*
> *say they should be tired because the Word of God tells us that He*
> *that findeth a wife findeth a good thing. We shouldn't be look-*
> *ing but rather loving on the Lord and being a "wife" to him and*
> *his purpose.*
>
> *(N.M.)*

During college, when I wasn't rushing home to see David, I spent as much time studying how to become a wife as I did physiology. Even though we were not engaged or even talking about marriage, I already began to see myself as the future Mrs. David. I saw myself cooking in his kitchen and sharing our combined hopes and dreams, while watching our children grow up before our eyes. He was my fairy tale and nothing was keeping me from it. The one thing that I've discovered is if you find yourself always going with the world's trend on marriage then you may need to evaluate if you really know who you are and whose you are. I studied everything on the Internet about a wife, the world's way, and attempted to combine Proverbs 31.

"Who can find a virtuous woman for her price is far above rubies…"

Proverbs 31:10

The world's view of marriage can never be for couples who have a relationship with God because that fellowship would have darkness rather than light. If the world isn't quoting God, then they quote its opinion.

I convinced myself that the more that I studied, the more attributes of this perfect "virtuous woman" I was gaining. I wanted someone to love me and validate who I was as a woman. The goal was to be a wife and I would bypass the process for the prize.

Don't bypass the process for the Prize! Before we go forward let's stop. If you are in a relationship with someone, it's ok to take your time. I don't care how many people around you are getting married, engaged or in long term relationships take your time. There is a process that can't be avoided if you want a successful marriage.

Let's take a field trip.

In the book of Esther there was a king that had several wives. One was wives Vashiti. She refused to come to a banquet that King Ahasuerus was hosting. He was furious and she was removed from her position. After a while, he began a search for a new group of women that would join his harem. The king was looking for a new queen. Several women were brought to the kin, including Esther, who found favor in the sight of the king. She was selected to go through 12 months of purification, six months of oil of myrrh and six months of perfumes and sweet spices. Oil of myrrh is multipurpose and expensive oil. It was used in many ways in Biblical times. One use was to purify. The oil tasted both bitter and pungent, but smelled of vanilla. Once the king found that he preferred Esther it was merely the beginning. No matter how eager she was to spend time enjoying the benefits that came with her title she had to be cleansed. Esther on the outside had all the qualifications to take her rightful place. She was beautiful and obviously she had the capability of being submissive.

What am I saying???

Your beauty doesn't qualify you as a potential successful relationship candidate.

Your great job doesn't qualify you as a potential successful relationship candidate.

Your educational background doesn't qualify you as a potential successful relationship candidate.

Your bank account doesn't qualify you as a potential successful relationship candidate.

The qualifications of being a potential successful relationship candidate include, but are not limited to: being whole and complete whether you're in a relationship or not, allowing God to cleanse you from your past hurts, disappointments and pain, understanding your own limitations, having a clear understanding of your purpose. The journey is difficult but the process is well worth the effort. If you read further, Esther, as a result of allowing herself to go through the process, was able to free her people using the favor and courage she had obtained in her patience.

I had the misconception that David would complete me. I felt like I wasn't whole alone. I learned was that in order to have a successful relationship I had to be whole first. He and I equaled happiness and freedom from the sentence I had pronounced on my life. NEWSFLASH: No one, whether male or female, can compensate for your lack of esteem. It is no one else's responsibility to confirm your identity. If you are unsure of whom you are, then don't get into a relationship. I couldn't ask someone to compensate for my lack of esteem and confidence. I needed to know who I was in God.

The idea of being a wife seemed easy to me, loving someone wasn't hard and who better to love than the man that taught me weekly at a home Bible study. I admired him, in a way I looked to him as a mentor. He prayed several times a day, kept the Sabbath and fasting was a part of who he was. He was everything I thought I wanted in a husband.

What is a husband? Although the Bible clearly states what the picture of a good wife and a bad wife entails, it is far less descriptive of what a husband looks like. On the outside, David looked like a doting boyfriend, compassionate, loving and the strong silent type. He sent me my favorite oatmeal pies and ramen noodles and gave me $25 a week. I know it doesn't seem like much, but on the weekend he would travel two hours to Albany State University and drive me back to his beautiful home. We would go on long walks where he would whisper how much he loved me and that we belonged together. Together we participated in several youth events and I never tired of watching David teach and preach to young people. I was most intrigued by his knowledge of the Word. He was a man of mystery and the more mysterious he was, the more I wanted to know. He could make me laugh so hard during the hard days. He gave me the attention that I strongly needed. Although we were heavy in the church, we struggled deeply in our flesh. We believed our foundation was secure but no matter how great our intentions, we built our future in sin. It doesn't matter how you try to dress it up, sin is sin. I would love to place all the blame on David for our lack of restraint, but I take equal responsibility. We were consistently putting ourselves in positions where we were alone with little else to occupy us but our affections and lustful desires. Somewhere, during the months that we were talking about how we wanted to conquer the world in the ministry, we crossed the boundary into fornication. Yes, I loved David very much, but I loved the physical part of our relationship as much. We made the mistake of confusing the love and passion in our relationship for the magnetic attraction of the lust in him drawn to the same in me. It's crazy that we researched every scripture about how to minister to young people how to help them in their daily walk, but couldn't research the scriptures to help us control our flesh and ultimately be delivered from it. We thought that the answer to our lack of restraint was a marriage license. We discussed our weakness in our flesh during dating but with little resolve when all we needed to do was go to God and truly repent to turn away from sin. We will ask God to restore our relationship with Him. Restoration in Him would have restored our relationship's foundation. Our chances of reclaiming our union would have been more successful.

My world was perfect. He loved me and I loved him. That was all we needed, we thought. When we came across people who didn't believe in us, we just chalked it up to their misunderstanding or misguided vision from God.

He Says the Words Every Woman Dies to Hear... 2

The moment was fast approaching when David and I needed to make a life decision. We were becoming increasingly uncomfortable about witnessing to our youth department because of our own private failures in our flesh. We were spending most of our free time together. During one group Bible study in his home, his mom and I had an argument. I was in complete awe of how she had changed over the course of months.

She and I were in the kitchen talking. I sensed a change in the demeanor and tone of her conversation. She had turned from the sweet loving woman to a woman scorned. She began to act jealous at David's sudden shift in attention toward me.

After Bible study, she and I ventured off to the deck as we had done many nights before. It was on this deck that she opened up about some personal moment of pain and I shared up about some scars.

"Last night, Nadia, I had a dream about David. He was married," Mama said cold and distant. She looked up into the darkness, not saying much. The tension was so heavy and thick you could slice it into pieces.

"Wow Mom, are you ok with that?" I asked hoping for an answer that gave us her blessing. Strangely, I believed that I had already received her permission. The fact that her son, the good son, the one she depended on for everything was slipping from her fingertips was troubling and she was very open about it. After many years, I can honestly say I understand how that must have felt.

"All I saw where her hands and tonight I looked at your hands and they were hers," she said.

With that she rose from her chair and walked into the house. I stood there with a mixture of excitement and dread because it was obvious that she wasn't ready to let him go. I reminded myself of her previous words months ago but since that time something had changed. What had begun as Bible study, ended in us trying to pray a spirit out of the house. Very emotional about having to go through that kind of ordeal, I told him that maybe we were wrong about us being meant to be together. I thought maybe it would be best if we took some time apart. As I was preparing to leave, he walked away to his room looking defeated and became very angry and destroyed his room out of his frustration. In seconds he had flipped his mattress over, broken his trash can and bent the railings under his bed.

Now, at this point we must pause. A wise person once said, "if a person shows you who he is, believe him." I tried to calm him down but he was very angry and disappointed. This I understood, but his loss of control worried me greatly. He said between tears that he knew we should be together. During the six months of our relationship, I had never seen this part of David's personality. My best friend Keisha saw that I was obviously shaken up and we had seen enough so she dragged me out of the house. Against his objections she took me home.

A while after arriving home, the phone rang and looking down at the screen on the caller ID. I knew it was David. I thought for a few minutes before I answered it. I had been pacing the floor at Keisha's wondering what was next. I had invested myself into a man that has family issues and a temper. I wasn't sure about our future, but I was sure that since this type of outbreak was unusual that if David had a happier relationship, then he wouldn't be as upset. I knew how I felt about him, but I also knew that going up against his mother was a fight I wasn't ready for. He apologized to me for his horrible outburst and behavior and that's when it happened. He said the words every woman dies to hear "Nadia, I don't have anything but my love for you, will you marry me?" I was floored even in the midst of my turmoil I knew that David was my best friend. Tears welled up in my eyes and I said yes. I believed that the bedroom incident was isolated and wouldn't happen again right? Wrong.

I began to come home every weekend and stay at his home. By the end of my first semester, our relationship took another turn.

"Hey babe, I think we need to talk" he said hesitantly, on a ride home from school.

"What's wrong? Everything ok with your mom and sister," I asked concerned as he had seemed distant the last week, not returning my calls right away and not talking much.

"Yes. I've been thinking a lot about our relationship and what is the best thing for my family and you," his voice seemed to crack a little and as he neared the end of his words his voice seemed low as a whisper.

"What is it? You know you can tell me anything. Is this a 'friend moment,'" I kept pushing. We had a code word for anything we said that a girlfriend or boyfriend would normally be against. We called it a friend moment and anything that is discussed during this moment couldn't be brought up during relationship conversation or disagreement.

"It's just that being with you has caused me a lot of strain and I just think that we need to end this before we go too far. I'm not good at talking and I wrote everything down in the letter in the glove compartment with all the answers you might need.

"What? Are you kidding me?" I said, shocked. "After all I've had to endure over these last few months and how my parents keep fighting me about seeing you on the weekends. You're breaking up with me in the car?"

The tears began to well up in my eyes and my anger was lifting every time I thought about it. Reluctantly, I dug in the glovebox and under the papers was a little felt box that held the promise of his love.

"Nadia, I love you. I want to know will you marry me?" he asked, as we drove back from Albany.

"Yes, of course I will. Don't you scare me like that" I asked wiping the unnecessary tears from my eyes. I couldn't help but leap across the seat and give him the biggest kiss ever. He was cracking up at me about to go crazy. I wore his ring like it was a permanent band around my heart. A few weekends later, as I was visiting Atlanta, I opted to stay with my parents. I told them about my engagement and being the good parents they are, they warned me that I was making a mistake. They supported me in every crazy decision of my life, but marriage was a little over the top.

After unsuccessfully enlisting in the Navy, I had taken a year off and worked two jobs. They believed that David was a phase, like my taste in wide leg pants and mushroom-styled hair. My first semester in college I had a 3.5 grade point average and they thought I was throwing it all away for some boy I barely knew. They told me I should stay in school and if this boy was truly the one, then he would be there for me after my degree. Then they would plan us a huge wedding. Starting college was the first time in my life that I went with my parent's opinion instead of against it. Of course, I thought that my parents were only trying to control my life and they didn't understand who I really was. Besides they didn't know God's plan for me. They were just my parents how could they know anything about my life when I was the one living it.

Well I'm sure you know what I should write here!

WRONG! WRONG! WRONG!

The worse thing happened about the beginning of my marriage with David was that we ran off and eloped. Yes, literally I woke up one morning and David told me that I was to be ready to leave and go out of town when he returned from work. I got up in anticipation of us finally making our commitment official, put on my favorite dress and waited for David to return home. I knew I wanted someone that would support me, so I called my best friend to witness. We traveled to Alabama where I met David's aunt who changed my world forever. Before a justice of the peace and God, I pledged that I would love and respect David for better and worse. I didn't see the fact that I had made a mistake and it would come sooner than later.

I had gone to sleep the night before with little responsibility and stress and woke up in the arms of my lover and best friend who was now my husband. After such a joyous time we had to return to reality the fact was that we had to tell our parents we were now husband and wife. The way that I told them was perhaps the most challenging part of our confession. My mother had invited us over. On the way there I told David that I thought that we should tell my parents. I knew they would be disappointed but I knew it was necessary. The longer we waited the more hurtful it would be. My mother sat me down and told me that she believed that living with this boyfriend of mine was wrong. Christ would not bless our union if we were in sin, the only thing I could say was that I was actually married to the man she thought was my boyfriend. Let me be the first to tell you that I am the only girl and my parents' baby. You can only imagine what kind of reaction my parents gave us when we came back from Alabama married. What I will say is that my parents, although extremely disappointed in my decision, did their best to support us. After the initial shock, they embraced my husband as their own son.

Who Am I, Really? 3

Who is a wife? What does a wife do? These are questions for everyone has made their own answers. No matter who you asked, they couldn't give the definition, just an opinion or their own horror story of a bad marriage. A church friend gave me, as a wedding present, a dust pan and broom telling me that these were necessary tools for a wife. Another explained that I could have sex anytime now, as she could with her husband. So from these enlightening moments I gathered that cleaning and sex with my man were key ingredients in a marriage. Growing up my mother who was more dominant than my father gave me the impression that combining force with your request was also an attribute of being a wife. My father was the strong silent type leaving in my eyes everything to my mother's capable hands.

Going about my normal routine I began to be what I thought a wife was, pulling my interpretations and mixing them with what I read and what I heard from other wives. I got up every morning at 6 a.m. to cook breakfast for my husband. Laid his underwear in the bathroom and made sure when he arrived home the house was clean and I was beautiful for him. Now, I am not saying that a wife should not take care of her husband, especially one that allows her to stay at home while he supports the family, but if your reverence for each other is not based on your love for God and your spouse, but is based on what other people think, the relationship is not genuine. This "Barbie" Nadia, the woman with no identity, existed for only a short time perhaps only a few months. Until the day I went to the mailbox and what I found inside ultimately would change our perfect world.

I made it a point to never read my husband's mail, so I just laid the envelopes close the bed and went about my daily routine. I was proud to be Mrs. David. Our marriage was no longer a secret, so I was free to tell everyone of my happiness. Shortly after the arrival of the letter, I was cleaning up our bedroom and saw the letter lying on the floor. It looked important but from the way that David left it scattered on our floor, I assumed it was not. I picked up the thick letter and sat on the edge of our bed and read the words out loud

"Your home will be auctioned off in foreclosure due to nonpayment."

I couldn't believe what I was reading, so I read it again out loud but no answers came to me other than foreclosure isn't something that happens all of sudden. I knew it had to be a process.

I began to pace back and forth in the house as the tears welled up in my eyes. As the moments passed waiting for my new husband to come home. I was losing all the trust I had. My perfect husband was slowly showing signs of cracks that had obviously been there all the time but I must have ignored the signs. I went down my checklist: Good Christian, check; attractive, check; job, check; no baby-mommas, check, honest man, check–I hope!

He came in as usual and kissed me at the door. Our kiss was tense and he could tell something was wrong.

"Hey babe what's wrong?" he said, coming in taking off his shoes, as he noticed there wasn't anything cooking.

"What does that letter that was on the floor on the side of the bed mean?" I looked up at him.

"What letter are you talking about?" he asked. All I could think was that he was that he was clearly joking.

"When were you going to tell me David?" I asked him in the most accusatory tone I could muster. I watched his face change from love to defense. I watched as my husband searched for the words to explain, but found none and resorted to blame. Gone were the words dripping with romantic overtones. I was angry and becoming more so as the moment passed with no rebuttal. The only words he could muster was how he had spent so much coming up and down to Albany and giving me money that he had neglected to pay the mortgage. He looked ashamed not from his lie, but from the look of hurt and mistrust he was beginning to see in his new bride. Too ashamed to admit his imperfection shattering the dream that he was my prince charming, he had hidden our family's impending foreclosure. He had mishandled his money for the last few months trying to give me everything I asked for and didn't want to trouble me with the details of the house issues. I'm not sure if the outburst that followed our talk was the first or second since our wedding but now our fights included broken glass, holes in the walls and broken promises. Unfortunately, there was little to be said because to say that I was ignorant in the matter of bill paying was an understatement. I barely understood how to manage a checkbook, so I wasn't much help in the way of budgeting or managing money. One of the most important things to learn from this harsh lesson is that before couples marry, or even consider a serious engagement, each one must evaluate their own finances. It seems obvious that a person would have the practical skills of check writing, budgeting, money management and savings, but not always. Never be ashamed to ask or research how to better manage your singleness before branching off into relationships. The virtuous woman that many women seek to be had great money management skills.

"She considerate a field, and buyeth it: with the fruit of her hands she planteth a vineyard.

She girths her loins with strength, and strengtheneth her arms.

She perceiveth that her merchandise is good: her candle goeth not out by night.

She layeth her hands to the spindle, and her hands hold the distaff.

She stretcheth out her hand to the poor; yea, she reacheth forth her hands to the needy.

She is not afraid of the snow for her household: for all her household are clothed with scarlet.

She maketh herself coverings of tapestry; her clothing is silk and purple.

Her husband is known in the gates, when he sitteth among the elders of the land.

She maketh fine linen, and selleth it; and delivereth girdles unto the merchant.

Strength and honor are her clothing; and she shall rejoice in time to come.

She openeth her mouth with wisdom; and in her tongue is the law of kindness

She looketh well to the ways of her household, and eateth not the bread of idleness.

Her children arise up, and call her blessed; her husband also, and he praiseth her.

Many daughters have done virtuously, but thou excellest them all.

Favor is deceitful, and beauty is vain: but a woman that feareth the Lord, she shall be praised.

Give her of the fruit of her hands; and let her own works praise her in the gates"

Proverbs 31:10-31

The virtuous women was not only conscious of what her family had and needed but she was also an entrepreneur using the gifts God had given her to further her household. Another fact that is often left out about this ideal woman is that she knows who she is. She "perceives that her merchandise is good." She doesn't have to wait for someone to tell her that she is worthy, she knows it already because of her relationship with the Lord.

Girlfriend Note: ————————————————

> *Just for a moment, I want you to let just that marinate. She doesn't have to wait for someone to tell her that she is worthy, she knows it already because of her relationship with the Lord.*

She doesn't wait for her husband's opinion to validate her nor does she have to boast of her great skills but she does what is necessary for her family and looks for not reward in return. Her service is to God and her family. The Bible describes the virtuous woman's character and tenacity before it ever talks about her husband.

We all enjoy the story of the virtuous woman often feeling like we aren't ever going to measure up to this awesome woman of God, but I believe we can. If we take more time to be better stewards over our time, family, resources and money we can be as influential as this inspiring woman.

What you see is what you get...

David and I wouldn't have had many of the financial struggles if I had been more involved with the budget in our home. In marriage usually one spouse is stronger in one area than another, but we shouldn't expect one person to shoulder all the responsibility alone. It is very important that a couple recognizes who is stronger in the area of finance and the other parts of a relationship. In marriage, each has to know their role and what each brings to the union. Often we believe that bringing ourselves to the marriage is enough, but we forget that once a couple is joined in marriage they are joined in everything! Bills past, present and future, pay attention to how each handled their personal finances before marriage because will be the trend they carry into the union.

I had so many pent up frustrations and I felt very alone. I couldn't talk to my mother because marrying David had been my decision. My lack of preparation was the cause of my new found mistrust. Now, it's important to mention that while I was dealing with the stresses of upcoming foreclosure and not knowing where we would live, my mother-in-law and sister-in-law were also living with us. Yes, the woman that had grown from loving me to pure hatred overnight resided with us. She told my husband that I was the worse woman alive. The sister, now also swore that some whore had stolen her brother from her. I had interrupted their live with David and I was the third wheel. Let's just say the family and I weren't seeing eye-to-eye. I felt betrayed, to say the least. I cried as I watched my husband allow his mother to call me every name in the book and his sister disrespected me on numerous occasions just because they could. He never defended me. He was caught between his love and devotion for his me and respect for his mother and sister. He was obligated to take care of them because he had brought them to Atlanta from Florida. He seemed to feel that he couldn't desert them especially since this was his second marriage. What's worse is that instead of helping the family and I build a relationship, David watched as they tore our marriage down. I was his wife right? He had chosen to love and cherish me right? Leave his mother and cling to me, the wife, right?

Now that I can look back at the beginning of our marriage, I see so many mistakes that led us down the path of no return. One of the first mistakes was that during our courtship, we never discussed our financial plan, never spoke about the living arrangements with his family or my inclusion into his world. That's not his fault, it's mine. Don't get me wrong, marriage is a beautiful institution paralleling Christ and the church, but if not planned correctly, the implementation can be doomed before the start. In my idealistic fairy tale of marriage, I had never included how to handle fights or disagreements, so as the stresses increased and so did the verbal attacks toward one another. I say to anyone who is planning and contemplating marriage, have a clear concise plan drawn out for at least the first five years. You can't plan for everything, but having spiritual direction keeps you focused on the vision God intended for you to carry out. The Bible speaks plainly about having a vision in *Habakkuk 2:2*:

> *"And the Lord answered me and said, write the vision, and make it plain upon tables, that he may run that readeth it."*

The Lord understood that when you write the vision down it brings life to it, it's a written confirmation of the things a couple needs to accomplish. The word also speaks about the consequences of no vision in *Proverbs 29:18*:

> *"Where there is no vision the people perish ..."*

This scripture is not only related to a man or woman's spiritual life but also marriages. The reason for the plan is simple, it keeps order. We serve a God that only functions in order and not chaos and if confusion arises, God is most definitely not involved. So brides, I admonish you to know what plan your husband has for the finances to how and when you will start a family, provided you haven't started one yet. Being aware of each other's financial history may seem excessive, but when it comes to trusting each other in your marriage, it is a necessary evil. The Bible says in *Matthew 19: 5-6:*

> *"For this cause shall a man leave father and mother, and shall cleave to his wife: and they twain shall be one flesh?. Wherefore they are no more twain, but one flesh. What therefore God hath joined together, let not man put asunder."*

This means exactly as it's written that the two are made one flesh that means not just in the areas that you want to include them but in EVERY way. Even discussing how we were raised plays a significant part in marriage.

Girlfriend Note: ─────────────────────────

> *Before you decided to marry or get into a serious relationship make sure that you are mentally, spiritually and emotionally ready to carry the responsibility that involves being one flesh. Marriage is difficult enough without both parties considering the realities of joining families, finances and personalities.*

If your spouse was raised in a home where money was never scarce or the perception of money wasn't strict, then he or she will be more frivolous with money. Or if there was financial strain in his or her household growing up, then his perception of money will be more restrained, which would cause problems if there is no communication. It is so critical to have this discussion during the engagement process, because after the marriage it is too late. As closely as the husband watches the way that his future wife cooks and cleans, the bride must also watch the way he manages his own household because habits are formed and don't just happen in relationships.

Now back to the story...

My husband decided it would be best, in order to save the house, to file bankruptcy. We were beginning to breathe and the strain in our home became slightly easier. His mother and sister also decided to leave. Our relationship had turned extremely strained and I welcomed the decision. It was the first time in our life that we were alone just the two of us. I cherished getting to know David without the pressures of trying to impress his mother. David and I had just started working together at a restaurant.

One day a few month's later, while we were out enjoying each other, his phone rang. The person on the other end wanted David and I to take full custody of his sister Alicia. The details were foggy, but the conclusion was that David would have to assume responsibility for his sister because his mother was having some life difficulties. We were about to add to our already tumultuous relationship a menstruating teenage girl with strong opinions and an attitude. I was extremely worried. Our lives instantly became more complicated. I struggled with the reality that I was responsible for a twelve year old girl and I myself was only 20. She was a beautiful opinionated young teen who helped me grow up fast. After a few run-ins, she became the best friend a young woman could have. Although David and I took on this new challenge with love and dedication, it was a hard transition for us emotionally. We began to fight again so our highs were high and our lows were worse than the deepest pit of hell. Alicia was there to witness it all.

I wanted to trust him, but I couldn't. All I could remember was seeing those papers and how he lied to me while we dated. But the reality wasn't just that he lied, it was that I lied to myself. I had created a fantasy that I had accepted as reality. Marriage is hard, but a bad marriage is barely tolerable. Once two people have lost trust in each other, it's not long before it spills over in every area of their life. My mistrust in my husband's ability to budget our finances was growing tremendously every day. He, too, was also developing a level of mistrust because he felt like the one person who had been a constant emotionally toward him in the last few months was slowly turning her back and I imagine that he felt alone. As much as we were committed to each other, it was as if the stresses and strains of our finances were the subject of every conversation and argument. Instead of supporting my husband's dreams of becoming an entrepreneur, I drove him to work. After such a hectic transition in our finances early in our marriage, I was afraid to leave anything to chance. I needed a tangible dream while he believed if God gave him a vision for our family, He himself would assure its success. I want to say that I wanted something that was definite but David thought that his ideas came from God. I didn't trust his insight on the vision of God. He had apologized for the mistakes he had made in the beginning, but with no trust in a relationship how could we be successful. I learned how important it is to forgive! My unwillingness to forgive my husband caused me to act in ways that didn't give reverence to him, rather it showed disrespect.

I challenge wives reading this to give their husbands room to believe. Even allowing him to fail is a part of trusting the leadership God has granted to him. Now that doesn't give the husband the right to deceive his wife. Communication is very important to a marriage's success. Remember God can't fail. The Word says that he is incapable of lying, for instance in *Numbers 23:19*:

> *"God is not a man; that he should lie neither the son of man that he*

should repent hath he said, and shall he not do it? Or hath he spoken, and shall he not make it good."

If the Lord has promised you and your spouse a specific thing, it's important to not look at your circumstance and doubt. The longer you doubt the vision, the longer it takes for it to come into existence. When you doubt the vision in essence you doubt the visionary, which is not your husband but the Lord. I speak to you not only as woman of God but a woman that forfeited what God would have given David and me because it looked impossible. Sometimes you have to take a step back and remember all the times God brought you out of situations that were impossible and remind your spirit that nothing is impossible for God.

When speaking of trusting your husband completely, I'm sure you're thinking but what if I know that he's doing the wrong thing and I see him failing? The first step is to go into prayer. Let your warfare be done on your knees and not with the things the Word calls "an unruly evil" that is untamable. Your words can be like lethal weapons to your husband's pride if used incorrectly. The Word says in *Proverbs 18:21:*

"Death and life are in the power of the tongue."

The Lord created your husband and who better to give him direction than the One who made him. I remember instances in my marriage when David would say something to me about some new idea he had and I would just become angry and start and argument. Never taking the time to take in what he was saying and asking one simple question "Honey, did you pray about that?" If the answer is yes and my spirit is still at odds, then I should have gone into prayer asking God either to bring peace to my spirit or show my husband a better way to accomplish the task at hand. It's all about taking a time out to focus in on what God is doing and hopefully if we've been in prayer the way we should then our home is one accord and the plan of action is executed.

God has trusted wives with power to intercede for the husband, as he is the head of the home. If the marriage is to be successful wives must pray daily for the vision and trust God's voice is the only one the husband yields to. Now if your husband is not saved, the Word doesn't give you an option not to submit, so continue to draw him in love and remember that you were once on the side he was and it took the love in one of God's people to bring you to Christ. If you continue to live upright before Him, he will wonder why you seem happier than he does, or why it's so easy for you to treat him like a king when he treats you like a pauper. Sometimes the harsh reality is that we don't seek God approval for our mates before we marry. After we figure out that we've made a mistake, we run to God and for permission to get out of it. Where was God when you were writing up the invitations, spending the money on cakes and dresses? The Bible says that if we continue to ask for something and God sees we want it that he is like a father that will give to us. Look at the story in *Samuel 8:7* about the people of Israel that asked Samuel for a king to rule and God allowed Saul to be king over the people. Now, I know you're probably wondering how that relates to marriage well if you keep begging for something and God allows it to happen ask yourself can you really complain?

Proverbs 3:5:

"Trust in the LORD with all thine heart; and lean not unto thine own understanding."

Proverbs 3:6:

"In all thy ways acknowledge him, and he shall direct thy paths."

> *Don't lean on your own personal assumptions of emotions that*
> *can and will change, but rely on God who cannot lie or falter*
> *in all your life decisions.*

—————————————————————————————— •

No, God doesn't pick our mate, the man chooses the wife but he does say that if we would acknowledge him in all our ways then he would show the way to go. *Proverbs 18:22* states

> *"Whoso findeth a wife findeth a good thing, and obtaineth favour of*
> *the Lord."*

Something that we fail to see sometimes in this scripture is the reference to finding a wife Webster defines a wife as a woman acting in a specified capacity. Who is "she" married to, in whose favor is she acting? I ask you women of God that are preparing to marry or those that have already crossed that threshold, if you are ready to be the portal in which the favor or un-merited influence can come to your mate or are you going to be the negative force in his life. This is a question I wish I had asked before entering into a commitment to God and my husband. It's up to us whether we go the way the Lord leads but it is mapped out. I believe that's why the Lord sends us pastors to help us see the way or carry out that path. Before one can marry, it is imperative to go through marriage counseling because there may be some areas that are not addressed initially during the courtship that have to be settled before the "I do's." When we skip this necessary step as I did, then the surprises come creeping up that were unexpected and sometimes lethal.

You Can't Tell Me What to Do! 4

Who said that submission was an evil word that degrades and minimizes the power of a woman? I believe that society has crippled women by suggesting submission is in some way a sign of weakness. Why cater to your spouse when you make more money than he does or have more influence than him in society? Just the word alone often makes women cringe because along with it displays the picture of being beneath one's husband. I challenge this theory. It takes more strength to wait on God and believe in God's purpose in your husband than it does to just scream at him about the decisions he makes. Webster's defines submission as yielding to one another; the act of presenting for consideration, arbitration. What's wrong with allowing a man to be what he was created to be? It doesn't make me weak to allow the man of God chosen and designed for me to follow the plan God has orchestrated for every area of our life. Listen at the end of the day, if you don't treat your man right, that means knowing and being concerned with what makes him happy, content, healthy and fulfilled, then another woman is lining up to fill in the blanks. The truth is that a man needs to feel respected. He needs to feel like he's the king of the castle. Even when he doesn't act like it or feel like it, he needs to always feel like the woman he's chosen to share his life with respects his decisions, direction and his vision. Never get too busy to listen to him.

Now comes the part that no one really discusses—the yielding to our husband after he's upset us, we're tired or just plain not in the "mood." The best way to illustrate this is to show you my deception in regards to submission. In my case my emotional roller coaster was shifting over into the physical part of our marriage. I can't tell you how many nights I developed a headache or saw my withdrawal as some type of unspoken punishment. I ask you, if a man is supposed to do or give us something specific in order to win our intimacy or affection, how different are we than a prostitute? It was so hard to separate what was going on the outside of our bedroom with what should have been going on in it! It became a way to withdraw myself from him. It had gotten so bad that even subconsciously I denied him. We would wake in the morning and he'd tell me that I had fought him in my sleep without my recollection. I just laughed and apologized. I never considered how my denial of his affection actually began to tear down our already teetering union. I thought that lying beside him every night would seal my position as his wife and I was completely wrong! God already knew what happened to a man once he was denied so many times. I left my husband uncovered and just as cliché as it sounds made it possible for another woman to show interest in him. As much as I'm sure he loved me, her attention reminded him that he was still a "man." I had let him forget with my harsh words and lack of attention.

First Corinthians 7:5: "The wife hath not power of her own body, but the husband: and likewise also the husband hath not power of his own body, but the wife Defraud ye not one the other except it be with consent for a time that ye may give yourselves over to fasting and prayer and come together again, that Sa-

tan tempt you not for your incontinency {through your lack of restraint of sexual desire amplified}...

The Lord created us with certain desires that are fulfilled through our flesh and completely permissible within marriage. He understood that once the union of marriage was consummated and the spouse didn't meet these desires, that the enemy hones in on that void and attempts to quench it through carnal attractions or rather distractions. As time went on, my subconscious behavior transcended into my natural life and I began to detest his touch, his smell even his laugh all the things that I fell in love with suddenly annoyed me. The enemy is the king illusionist and I allowed him to deceive me into blowing up everything David did as an attack against me. I stopped doing things that we used to do together our game night (use your imagination). Our movie dates and even those spontaneous times became no more. I became more disrespectful in public and at home. Now taking his cue from me, he became more volatile and angry. His manageable anger and rage became intolerable. The yells turned into punches in walls, furniture and even my windshield. This was subject to his whims and his control. Instead of using the gift of prayer, I encouraged his rants with unforgiving words and bullets to his manhood. I diminished my beauty to him and became the object in which brought him pain and turned him into a monster. Imagine this...

Everyone has heard of the classic story of Beauty and the Beast.

Imagine if Belle spent months nurturing and loving the beast. Under the stars reading each other poetry and gazing into each other's eyes. After all that time confessing their undying love for one another and the love broke the hideous curse from the beast and he is restored to the man that she wants. Imagine if she turned around the next day after the credits rolled (got the ring and the last name) and said "I can't stand you," "you're an ugly man" or even "I would rather go back to my other life before I met you" and the man turned right back into the monster that kept him bound hostage in that castle all alone and angry.

It wasn't until my separation that I truly saw what I did to God's man, one who was made and designed by God and not me. I have to reiterate that it's important to remember ladies even though we've been given the honor or marrying extraordinary men we did not create them. Contrary to popular belief and "Cosmopolitan," we can't change them. Only the creator God can. He is the only one that knows the true heart of a man.

Protect Your Marriage

This was the hardest chapter for me to write. When the Lord told me to write this one, it made me wonder what people would think about me? What would they think about my journey and my decisions? After all that thought and imaginations of backlash, I decided who cares! I care about each individual that picks up my book; I care about each life that will be directly affected by my honesty and care about the marriages that will be saved after I share with you my personal struggles.

Now with that introduction out of the way here goes!

You have to protect your marriage from three things: Other people, even if they are Christians, outside influences and ungodliness. I will illustrate all these things in my own life and how they ultimately led to the mistrust and deterioration of my marriage.

I know you're asking why can't I talk to my Christian friend about my marriage. She gives great advice. Well I'm not saying you shouldn't, just be mindful and sensitive to the Spirit of God who will lead you in all truth when discussing personal matter with your friends about your marriage. I remember a particular friend that I often shared troubling facts about my deteriorating marriage and how she was so sympathetic, always wanting to help. Unknown to me, one week after I left my husband she had moved in.

WOW!

The other problem is that when others give you their advice it's just that! It's an opinion based on the skewed facts that you've given the person which can be dramatically affected one way or another depending on how they feel about your marriage, your life and you. The very person that always wants to play audience to your drama may in fact be the one lining up to take your place. Beware of your associations! *First Corinthians 15:33* states *"Do not be misled: "Bad company corrupts good character."*

When I got married I was 19 years old, full of energy and life and most of my friends were single. People my age were in their second year of college, partying and being independent. I was a youth pastor's wife, taking care of my teen sister-in-law and her troubled mother. I was desperate to get out and hang with people with less responsibility and less stress.

WRONG!

When you spend time around a lot of people that don't share your same ideals and morals, one of two things will happen—either you will change them or they will change you. In my case, I started wanting to hang out with my single, borderline-saved friends. The definition or borderline-saved is going to church on Sunday all other activities other days of the week.

I watched their independence, their ability to hang out late at night with a different guy and have a new experience. I started saying to myself, "I'm missing something. There is this secret single society that I am not privy to because I'm married to Jesus' first cousin and he just won't let me do anything." The small seed was planted and, before I knew it, I was being totally rebellious to everything I knew in God and His Word. I started doing things I knew weren't right. What's not right? Outside influences!

I became addicted to all things sexual. Now I know many of you are reading this and wondering what that means. Well it means that most of my thoughts and actions were controlled by my sexual desire. I've since discovered that my lack of self esteem was the biggest reason for my problems. I associated sex with love and the more I did it and the 'freakier" I was the more love I thought I would receive. Once that theory didn't work, after about 20 years, I turned inward. If no one could love me the way that I needed, then I would just sexually please myself. You and I know this action as the word masturbation. Recently I found out that I was given a special gift in my bloodline that for which I didn't ask! I was watching pornography everyday and had love paraphernalia to keep me occupied. Most of this behavior was taking place without my husband's knowledge or participation. It was like any other addiction. It started out as something to tide me over until my marital intimate time and turned into an uncontrollable insatiable appetite for pleasure. I would often convince myself that my actions were normal and because I was married that I exempt from punishment. What I didn't know was that I was inviting a spirit in my relationship called Lasciviousness. Lasciviousness is defined as an uncontrollable desire for lust. The Bible describes this condition as greediness.

Ephesians 4:19 says *"Who being past feeling have given themselves over unto lasciviousness, to work all unGodliness with greediness."*

In the Amplified bible it reads *"..in their spiritual apathy they have become callous and past feeling and reckless and have abandoned themselves to unbridled sensuality, eager and greedy to indulge in every form of impurity, that their depraved desires may suggest and demand."*

The Bible teaches us that the wages of sin is death. In *Romans 6:23* says *"The payment and compensation is death"* but we often think that that death is literal and it can be but more often it is the spiritual death similar to the feeling that Adam an Eve may have felt being evicted from the garden. It separated me from God and made it less and less possible for me to feel the love He desperately wanted me to feel.

I'm sure you're wondering how a super saint like myself could struggle from this heavy sexual addiction and still be working in the church. I think it's because while the church speaks about how to get wealth, get back what the enemy stole and how not to kill your kids and husband they leave out a great detail how to be delivered from sexual addiction. We offer marriage as a remedy for lack of restraint and fornication and silence for all other addictions. We follow the "don't ask, don't tell policy." Often until someone influential in media, music or ministry speaks about it. Quietly, people like me raise our hands begging God to heal us, but we do not know what the steps are to being healed from this torment. The process isn't easy. If you can get through the first overwhelming urge, then each time you will get stronger and stronger. If you fall, don't beat yourself up but rather repent. Get up and keep moving. Don't allow yourself to stay in the place of condemnation.

I learned a few things about why masturbation and pornography can be two of the most deadly forces in a marriage. Number one masturbation teaches "I get my pleasure from myself." It disinclines a partner and can create feelings of resentment. Masturbation, although it is generally engaged in alone, often, because of the shame attached, involves others. In order for a woman to reach climax or orgasm without penetration or clitoral it must come from a thought or memory. That memory, sexual or not, must stimulate an arousal and build up tension inside the intimate places and then plateau. The media and several Internet self-help sites teach us that this behavior is normal and necessary to know one's body. This is a trick from the enemy! Anything that replaces the beauty of the intimate time in marriage designed for the sanctity of marriage is wrong. God designed a husband to know his own wife intimately thoroughly and never says that one should turn inward for pleasure.

After doing a lot of research I found out some shocking details, according to Adult Video News, in 2006:

Women keeping cyber porn viewing activities a secret 70%

Women struggling with pornography addiction 17%

Percentage of visitors to adult websites who are women 1 in 3 visitors

Women accessing adult websites each month 9.4 million

Women admitting to accessing pornography at work 13%

It's not just men who struggle with sexual perversion a many of women also suffer from this tormenting spirit. I spent many nights, after a wonderful night with my husband, trying to continue to pleasure myself. I knew that I had a problem, but I was too ashamed to tell someone about my secret addiction. If you are struggling in this area it is very important to pray and consult God about whom you can talk to and receive counseling because God does not desire for you to be controlled by anything, least of all your flesh. He said in his Word that He came to this world to die so that we may receive Liberty and be free. I also want you to know that although this desire may have tried to take you over. I declare that once you've read this that you will be honest with yourself and God. You will no longer struggle in this area. You are not alone! Even if your church hasn't dealt with this pressing issue, in the House of God it is being addressed somewhere. Don't cry another night because of your pain. You can be healed. This addiction cost me a lot of time with my husband because along with it came another spirit, perversion. The spirit of lust comes out in different ways. So now I had decided because of my own issues that my husband couldn't quite get me to the point that I needed. Maybe the only one that could truly satisfy me was another women. Even though we were in spiritual and physical disarray, I decided that if we had something to occupy our time maybe spicing up our sex life was the way to stop my constant need for outside sexual excitement. I can image now that my husband doubted himself sexually because of my lack of regard to him pleasuring me. In my husband's quest to satisfy me, we decided to add to someone to our relationship. In case you didn't know there is a secret society of individuals that add others to their intimate time in an effort to increase their pleasure. I want to stop here and say this: all that you need intimately, physically spiritually the Lord has put in your husband or wife. You and your spouse know what you need to satisfy the other and if you don't, then there has to be a level of communication in that area so one doesn't become resentful and look outside for the marriage for pleasure or satisfaction. The fact is the Lord doesn't give you permission to give anyone else your body or add anyone to the marriage covenant. This will create multiple problems and can hurt more than one person.

Saying this, I must also add that going into marriage you can't compare your spouse's intimate fingerprint (we will talk about the fingerprints in a latter chapter) with anyone else. They are unique and if you go into marriage with the idea that the last guy flipped you over, threw you down and rolled on the ground, you will be doomed intimately. The enemy has created a mirage of what sex should look like and it is not how God intended it to be. He has further convinced or bamboozled us into thinking that world's way to do things is the way we should conduct something God called to be Holy. This doesn't mean that you defile your spouse either. The definition of defiled according to Webster's Dictionary is to tarnish, dishonor shame and disgrace. This means that you should never pressure your spouse to do something sexually that they don't feel comfortable with. Christ commanded that we show benevolence, love and consideration of our own spouses in *Corinthians 7:3*. Remember although the Word says in Hebrew 4 that marriage is honorable is doesn't say it can't be tarnished by the things we do inside that marriage bed.

It's saying that we should keep the bed from being dishonored not anything we do in it can't be unholy. I believe the Lord leaves us with an interpretation of what should be held as holy or not but anything that causes shame to come upon either individual in that bedroom will dishonor your marriage. Remember misinterpretation of any commandment can lead you astray so if you're wondering what is holy or permitted in your marriage beds, please consult the Word of God. Remember that God doesn't give us a pass for ignorance, but rather tells us to seek him if we lack wisdom in any area. I want to make sure that I am not instructing you in this area further than pointing your attention the Word of God and prayer. Be careful whom you let speak to you in this area because many opinions or interpretations are varied. His or her personal ideas of what is permissible will be based on what happened in their bedroom and less about what the Word of God says.

Now back to the story … (this part is much harder for me to write than for you to read)

Pause. Breathe. Pause. Breathe.

Into my restaurant walked a 6-foot 1-inch woman dressed mainly like a man with short hair and I remember watching her come around the bar and my manager greeted her and explained that I would be training her while she was here. She was to learn all about the front of the house operation and I was her lucky teacher. From the moment I laid eyes on her I felt a strange attraction. Very similar to the feeling that I had when I first kissed my husband. It was weird. I had convinced myself that I wanted a woman. For months I couldn't pray, I couldn't bring myself to face God because I knew what I felt was wrong, but I didn't know what to do. I had stopped letting my husband touch me because his touch wasn't hers and when he did I imagined her. I never allowed myself to go any further than just my imagination and I am so glad that right before I hit the edge of the cliff, God stepped in and shook me. I remember being at a service and I coming to the place where I couldn't run anymore, I couldn't keep falling. I had to talk to God. I can't remember what he said, but what I can tell you is that I never had a desire for a woman again after that day.

Before I go on I need to stop and say a prayer for anyone that is struggling with perversion of any kind, masturbation, lasciviousness and recovering from sexual molestation. I want you to know something. God didn't mean for you to live in bondage to your flesh. He knows the pain you feel in the late night hour. Some times in my singleness, I would rock back and forth and cry out to God because the need to feel that intimacy was so overwhelming. I know that someone out there knows what that feels like, but I declare today after you read this prayer that you will no longer be subject to the whims of your flesh again.

Let's pray together:

"Father in the name of Jesus I thank you today. I thank you that your Word declares that we shall be free from bondage and sin and we thank you that you have protected us against all manner of disease and kept us alive by your grace. We know that it is only by your grace that we are here today and only because you love us that you didn't give us over to a reprobate mind for our continued abuse of what you created beautiful. We ask, You, God that you would forgive us of all sins knowing and un-knowing, for the homes we may have hurt because of our actions or the people that may have stumbled because of our lack of restraint. Father, we ask God that you teach us how to love ourselves and how to love others without using our sexual parts first. Teach us to treat our body a temple for your spirit because we know that you don't live in an unclean temple and Father please teach us how to value others bodies with the same regard as you do. We thank you that every wound that we have been in-

flicted with has now been healed because you took them upon you when you went to the cross. We forgive the one that first introduced us to this sin and the ones that may have opened the door for this perversion to lay doormat until it was ready to try to make us slaves to it. We denounce all powers of perversion at its root and from this day forward we will not be bound, from this day forward we are free from perversion and free from sexual sin and free from all acts that displease our Father. We love you and thank you in Advance that you will use our testimony to set others free. In Jesus name,

Amen.

If that touched you take a moment and destroy every work of the enemy. Discard the toys, burn the videos and delete the number. The Bible says in *Corinthians 6:18: "flee fornication and resist the devil and he will flee. But you have to want to be rid of Satan and his troupe of lies and antics."*

Now returning to our regularly scheduled program already in progress….

I also began to pray for a child as I thought that maybe what David and I were missing a little person with his daddy's smile and daddy's chocolate complexion. As ironic as it sounds I imagined that the cause of our division was because we were missing something more tangible to take our attentions away from our problems. I can tell you now that bringing a child into that kind of environment can be hard not only on the husband and wife but more importantly on the child. I thought down deep that I loved him and even through the fighting, I wanted desperately to have his child. We were not using birth control, but we were unlucky in our attempts to get pregnant. After complaining about abdominal pains David decided it was time to take a trip to the doctor. My doctor told me that I had too many cysts on my ovaries and that I wouldn't be bearing children as often as we had hoped. He instructed me to take birth control pills and eventually the cysts would shrink and we would conceive. We decided that it was unnecessary to take the pills because obviously it wasn't time to conceive and we were just starting to get our finances back in control thanks to our father in the ministry. Bishop Vinson. So we used no protection, I mean why use protection when we knew that we couldn't get pregnant, right? Wrong, once again. It was only a few short months later after I began to get sick and I knew something was definitely wrong when my normal helping of Stacked Border Nachos from On the Border sent me running to the bathroom instead of smiling with delight! A positive result from the little blue stick sent shivers and smiles throughout my body because finally my prayers were answered. I remember just prior to finding out that we were having a baby, David and I had one of the biggest fights of our marriage that ended up with me lying on the floor and him in regret saying "I can't believe this, what if you're pregnant?" Little did we know that I was already carrying a little surprise that would ultimately change our lives forever. After that the fights were not as intense. We had given each other some space and thanks to my new job title, corporate trainer, I spent less time at home and more time on the road. While I was away at a training session, I received a call from my David saying that one of the tests I had taken had come back and the baby tested positive for defects. According to the doctor there was no way to pinpoint what the defect was until I had an ultrasound. I rushed home on the next flight to find out that my son had a rare condition called gastrochisis. Gastrochisis is a condition where the intestines protrude through the outside of the abdominal cavity. I was devastated to say the least, after seeing a specialist he told us that either one or two things would happen. Either all of the intestines would be on the outside or a small amount. So the waiting game began.

Micah Andre's Story 5

After months and months of worry and trying to pretend that our little boy would be fine. On July 21, 2002, Micah Andre came bursting in the world by C-section. I remember the words from the doctor even now. "It's so little on the outside that I could have put it in." In my heart I already knew that this would be a hard road for Micah and for us. After he was born he was taken to a children's specialty hospital where he was immediately given surgery to repair his protruding intestines. I lay, heavily sedated, waiting for my husband to give me any news about our little boy. The call that I received was just what I dreaded. Micah had survived the surgery but in the process lost 90 percent of his intestines. His chance of survival was slim. We should be prepared for his shortened life. What's worse is hearing my husband telling me that he knew that our little boy would die. Via phone, he vented his frustration of pain and hopelessness as I lay praying that I would see my little boy again. I knew I couldn't give up God. God would not lie and tell me that he would give me a child and he would be healed in Jesus name. Every day until I could see my angel, I walked around that hospital praying and thanking God for my baby. I knew that things would be hard but I believe God said in his Word, and I believe it. He would not put more on me then I could bear. My husband's and my fights had reached an all time high because of the stress of not just having a child but now one who required special care. Neither of us could decide who would work and who would stay at home with our little prince. After much argument, I decided that I would stay home and it was just in time, because I found out that we were expecting another little one. So much for what the doctor had previously told us!

Micah spent much of his life in the hospital going back and forth. I spent as much time in the hospital bed with my son as I did in my own. Even though my little man was very ill, I could tell how excited he was about Mommy's big tummy and new baby coming. He would often kiss my tummy and I could tell that the children would be thick as thieves. In and out of the hospital with Micah we were so glad that Laila Grace came when he was at home with us. She was such a little blessing Micah loved her so much.

One day sticks out in my mind about the two of them. It was when she was just two months old, I had been out shopping with my mother-in-law and Laila, when we came home David told me he thought that Micah was probably sick because he had been sleeping all day. This was a sign of the usual infection. I put the car seat down on the floor to go to the kitchen and Micah got up and went over to his sister and kissed her and he went back over to the blanket to lie back down. David said that it was the first time that he had gotten off that blanket all day. I can only imagine what he was telling her in that kiss. The next day Micah went into the hospital with a common infection and never came home. During this visit, I saw my baby slipping away, he wasn't responsive to my touch anymore. All I could do was sing to him. We used to sing and dance in his room and cuddle in his huge bed together. I knew that he was just holding on for us. He was our miracle. No matter what the doctor said, we wouldn't concede to defeat about our lil' papa bear.

We had been waiting for the news from his primary gastro-intestinal doctor before we made a decision regarding his care. His doctor came back and told us that Micah chance of survival was slim and that even if he recovered he would eventually die from the complications in his liver. As result of his small gut he had to have TPN, which give the nutrients straight into his body. The medicine made to keep him alive was also killing his liver. His liver had so much damage from the continual use of the TPN that without a liver transplant he wouldn't live much longer. My husband and I knew this life was no way for our little boy to live. We made the calls and prayed together about what God would have us to do for our baby who was slowly slipping away.

We decided that as hard as it was that we would let our baby go home. I called Pastor Vinson and she herself had just come through a terrible sickness by the grace of God. She told us that she knew what it was like to be poked and prodded and no one should have to live like that. Through her healing, I had hope for Micah but God had already decided that Micah's journey was coming to an end. The next morning, we got to the hospital like normal and went about our normal routine with our son as they were weaning him off the pain medicine. With each hour he was becoming more coherent and I was able to give him a bath, the longest one he had ever taken. I sang to him and I told him that I would miss him, but he didn't have to hold on for us and he could go home and be with the Lord. After visiting all morning, I was exhausted I went into the waiting area to get some time alone. While I was there, I met a woman. We began to talk about parent life in the hospital and how hard it can be. She told me of her son who had died three times and had been revived. I told her about my angel who held on for 21 months, but in a few hours was going home to be with the Lord.

She began to weep and told me that she had been in the chapel praying and asking for a sign from God about whether to let her baby go or not. After hearing our story she finally knew it was time. I told her that it wasn't an easy decision but God had given us a release in our hearts. You never know why you go through what you go through while you're going through it, but God is allowing you to be testimony to someone else.

The time came for Micah to be taken off the machine which for two days had been breathing for him. We were able to pass our angel around for everyone to say their last goodbyes and thank God for allowing us to be able to have him with us as long as we did. I was the last to hold him and I told him what every mother would say, "Mommy would be fine and that I will miss you more than you could ever know." He reached his tiny hand up and touched my face and breathed his last breath in my arms. The room emptied and we made our memorial box. Discussion of disposal of his body, where we would bury him and the arrangements seemed like someone snatched my breath from my body, so I left the room for air. When the unit's doors opened, I was flooded with crying faces. I don't remember any of the faces except for my sister Shawn and a pastor from church telling me to breathe. I couldn't think that my little boy was gone and the kisses and the dancing songs. No more baseball hopes or football ambitions for him. He was gone and nothing any one could say could bring my little boy back.

Eventually, I did breathe again.

After his funeral I kept breathing mainly because I had a beautiful little girl named Laila Grace who lit up my world. She helped me breathe again and she helped me see that God loved me. I'm sure that you're saying, "How can a two-month-old do that when all she did was cry?" Well while she cried for me. I cried for her. She was truly sent from God and I thank God everyday for sending her to me. No one will ever replace Micah or even be close, but after months of bitterness toward the Lord I understood. I would love to say that I lost Micah, bounced right back and stood on the promises of God, but I didn't. I stumbled quite a bit because I couldn't understand why God took my baby and why he would allow David and I to go through so much at such a young age. There was a little secret between the Lord and I: sometimes when the Lord shows us things it's not to be discussed with anyone but simply to meditate. The lesson that I learned has made me a better woman.

I'm On Stage...
Lights Camera Action

6

Here comes reality crashing in. We were no longer two people consumed with the care of a special needs baby but two people unsure of who they were and more unsure of who they should be together. Before I address the pain that we endured as result of losing Micah, I want to briefly discuss something David and I didn't do that would have saved us a lot of pain, counseling. When two people lose a child, it can inadvertently bring about feelings of anger and resentment that can be directed at each other because it has no other place to go. Neither one of us wanted to blame the other or remain angry with God because he will never put more on us than we can bear, but it was hard not to. Counseling would have addressed the areas I had forced myself to hide during his death and bring David's to the forefront. Sometimes just knowing "absent from the body, present with the Lord" just isn't enough.

No, I'm not saying that the Word of God is not complete, but sometimes one's grief can be too great for them to even sit and comprehend the Word. Several of our friends told us that counseling was necessary, but we carried the super couple patch proudly on our chest in public. In private we were ripping each other apart. I remember David's Aunt Cecilia (you will hear all about her later, she helped me change my life) who had recently lost her husband in a car crash told us of how she replayed his funeral several times and had to go through therapy to deal with her deep grief. I believe that God was reaching out to us through her to start therapy. Had we undergone therapy during this rough period of our life, it wouldn't have been hard when the fits of rage began to get worse. I was so consumed by my own pain that David's pain meant almost nothing to me. It wasn't that I didn't care, it I was struggling daily with the stress of taking care of a beautiful baby girl and learning to live my life as mother of one now instead of two. Besides David seemed so in control all the time that he didn't need me. I think that was one of my biggest gripes with him was that he wouldn't let me in. I think he believed if he allowed himself to feel around me then I would treat him like he was weak, but in actuality had he shown me he needed me I would have felt like I could be vulnerable to him. *Ephesians 5:25* says, *"Husbands love your wives, even as Christ loved the church, and gave himself for it."*

I believe that sometimes becoming vulnerable to your spouse is like dying to yourself. A lot of men are reared with the theory that if he shows pain, then he's weak. He's taught that if he falls, then no one should see him cringe. Grit your teeth young man and take the stripes that life throws at you and the world will respect you. Ladies, we must be sensitive to our husbands in this regard, everyday our Black men are greeted with the stereotype that describes them as hustlers, drug dealers, drug addicts, and baby daddies. They walk around trying to prove to the world that they are not like every negative stereotype written. Many wear mean mugs like necessities and shields against rejections and disregard. Many even fall subject to the labels placed on them simply because they feel irrelevant and disrespected.

It's so important that when they come home that they don't experience the same rejection they sometimes experience in the world. There were very few times that David cried in front of me. I decided that he had probably found his closure about Micah the same way I did. We never really dealt with our issues and our relationship had become an illusion to other people and at home a satisfaction to our flesh when necessary. When a couple loses a child, even when it is expected, a piece of them leaves as well. In my case a lot of me left. I was hardly ever able to look at David because Micah had been the spitting image of him. After returning from a trip to gather our wits to Alabama, I came home with a little present. It was with mixed emotions that we embraced the thought of having another child. Micah had not been gone very long and our relationship was becoming more of a tolerance than love. I remember on the ride home that I told David that I didn't want to be with him and I was sure that our union was mistake even from the beginning. I ask myself now why couldn't I share my pain with him. Why couldn't I tell him that just being in his presence reminded me of the pain of losing my only son? Our son, the child that I prayed and asked God for, caused pain in his presence. During Micah's funeral people would come up to us and tell us how they knew couples who lost children that never survived a child's death. Somewhere along the way I adopted that theory as well. If you are in a relationship, never accept other people's fate for your marriage. Never let negative words be spoken over your spouse. I know that when we get into an argument, the automatic thing to do is to call our girlfriends and mothers and vice versa, but when we do we allow their spoken opinion to be like seed planted in a field. Once our anger is gone and we've embraced our spouse again, that doesn't remove the seed we've planted. Our words are powerful and we must use them to build up our spouses and not tear them down.

I allowed the pain of losing Micah to turn to hate for my husband. I'd love to say that he was completely at fault for this, but while he shares his part of the blame my lack of communication was really what ruined us. So as time went on, we became like two distant ships as it's told moving in different paths and only coming together in convenience. Don't get me wrong there were some very happy moments, but it seemed like the dark night outweighed everything good in David and me. I remember it like it was yesterday, that I was about seven months pregnant and attempting to be a better woman to David. I cooked breakfast for him on his birthday. It was becoming a rare occasion that we spent any time together because he was either working pretty late or spending his time on the computer playing games. I was fine with that because during this time I was reading more and just enjoying being me (something I should have embraced during singleness). During breakfast David seemed to have some sort of epiphany and told me that I was a good woman. He then went on to tell me that he had been engaging in conversation with another woman on the phone. I of course thought he was joking because although we had our problems surely he wouldn't be messing around while I was pregnant.

He assured me that they had only had a few conversations and that he was attempting to witness to her. Now this seemed unusual to me because David would direct women to me in ministry, because he didn't want his good spoken evil of. I wish I could say that I handled this like woman of God, gentle and loving but a few days later I erupted into a puddle of hysteria. I had never felt so betrayed in my life. All I could think is—I want out. Now this is really not about what happened that day but rather a simple way to explain that sometimes when we are so distracted with cares of the world that we look past things that are right in front of our face. I should have handled this situation with this woman immediately when I saw that she was attempting to make a connection with him (a few weeks prior she had shown up at a church function, shortly after that she called David's job asking for him). The enemy doesn't suddenly attack out of the blue. He is cunning and deceptive.

First Peter tells us to "be sober, be vigilant; because your adversary the devil; as a roaring lion, walketh about seeking whom he may devour."

The enemy doesn't rest. He's always looking diligently for a way to make the kingdom of God a lie. If I had been on my face praying for the man of God then I would have seen the enemy before he had an opportunity to strike so harshly. I left him open for the enemy's attack when I didn't fulfill those things that he needed from me especially so soon after we had lost our son. I was so consumed by my own pain and never once considered that although he was happy on the outside and appeared to be in control, he was hurting on the inside. Now saying all this doesn't give him the right or even the excuse to search out another woman but it does explain how she was able to slither in. I gave her an open avenue into my marriage when I began to ignore and mistreat my husband. She paid attention to him and listened to what his true desires were even the inappropriate ones that should have been shared only with his wife. She laughed at his jokes and the most important thing–she made time for him in her world when I was always to busy. While was busy consuming myself with church activities, my husband was allowing another woman to whisper sweet nothings in his ear.

———————————————•———————————————

Attention *"Wailing women,"* I know you feel like the church won't make it without you, it will! I know you're on the usher board, the deaconess board, women department head, and armor bearer and intercessor on first, third and fifth Sundays, but I warn you that if your house isn't taken care of, you are ineffective in any of your auxiliaries. Make sure that Daddy, kids and home are working before you join one more group. I know it's hard because you want to be busy for God but your home and family is your first ministry. Just make sure that you handle those first. They could be the thing that saves your marriage. So many times I chose a church activity over my husband's need to just lie at home in my arms. What you might not know ladies is that while you're away he's building a resentment toward you that's growing each day. He quietly suffers from neglect while he watches you give yourself over to everyone else in the church. You leave him to eat alone, and fall asleep in his bed first before you come in. Listen ladies, your man needs ministering to and not only in the sexual way but sometimes he just needs you to hold him. Caress him and whisper sweet nothings in his ear (whew! I just had to get that off my chest).

When a couple suffer the loss of child it's important because there is individual grieving, and their needs to be healing together too. We never healed as couple after Micah's death. I believe that was one of the many mistakes that led us to the arms of other people.

I know that as you read this you're probably thinking how you would have handled this. I ask you now to take a moment and think about the last time you told your husband what a wonderful man he is, even if you don't feel it. Or, when was the last time you surprised your husband with a candle light dinner, left a love note in the pocket of his jacket or telling him how he's the only man in the world for him. Or allowed him to tell you about his day before you rattle on about yours. I know that as women we have so many things pulling us from one second to the next but it's important that we remember that marriage is a ministry that deserves and needs our attention as just as much as everything else.

Now back to the story:

As I found out later, my husband and this woman had been engaging in several conversations that he had told me was to help her find salvation. Now, I wish I could tell you that I behaved as a lady and held my tongue, but I cannot. I went off on not just him but sent this young woman an e-mail detailing that her friendship with my husband was inappropriate and for her to discontinue it. I don't know that it was dissolved but David told me that it was.

Shortly after this I gave birth to our third child, Kayla Marie. By August I wanted out of our marriage. I had become very distant and so had my husband. What should have been a joyous time in our life was stressful and irritating. Never truly taking the time to understand my husband's need for another woman, I began to resent the fact that our vows meant little to him. I began to tear him down to my friends. I told anyone who would listen to my rants about my hatred for my no good husband. I would explain my unhappiness in the marriage.

Woe is me became a part of my adornment. Each day I was allowing myself to be a victim. Still not taking stock of what had brought David and me to this place. The first thing that I should have done is go into prayer asking God to first forgive me for the things I had done wrong to the man of God (because I had done so many). I should have asked Him to forgive me for losing sight of who created the man of God given to me. So many times I had gone to God telling him the things that my husband was doing wrong rather than asking God to change me! I was seeking Godly wisdom but not adhering to it.

In *Matthew 13:20-21*, it says, *"But he that received the seed into stony places, the same is he that heareth the Word, and anon with joy receiveth it; Yet hath he not root in himself, but dureth for a while: for when tribulation or persecution ariseth because of the Word, by and by he is offended."*

The amplified Bible describes tribulation as trouble or persecution comes then one stumbles at once. It's safe to say that I not only stumbled, but completely fell down hard.

My pastor told me that if I divorced my husband, I would regret it. God wouldn't be pleased. The Word speaks about divorce and why it was created in *Matthew 19:8, "...Because of the hardness of your hearts suffered you to put away your wives: but from the beginning it was not so."*

Divorce was only created because man's heart was hard. We had allowed the pain that surrounded our past to build up walls in my heart that only God could remove. It's so important if there has been any kind of mistrust in your marriage because of past indiscretions and you want your marriage to be what God intended, you must ask the unfailing God to heal you. If you don't, it doesn't matter if you divorce or not, you carry that mistrust and sometimes insecurity into every relationship in your life.

Back to the story:

My pastor and bishop told me to try to support my husband, sensing with each counseling session I became more distant and unreceptive. He asked me one question, "Did God tell you to leave your husband?" Of course he knew that God honors his Word and would never contradict his Word by telling me to leave my covering. I didn't understand, until now, what a covering truly meant. In order to understand what a covering is we must first examine the order of marriage according to the Word. In *Ephesians 5:23, "For the husband is the head of the wife, even as Christ is the head of the church: and he is the savior of the body."*

It's safe to say, that if the husband and wife are to be paralleled to the order of Christ and the church, then as Christ covers his church in love then the husband is to cover the wife in the same way. The Word even goes on to say that the love even extends into sacrifice. The way that Christ gave himself for His church, so should the husband love his wife as himself? And, if there was any doubt on how that love should be shown, the Word says it should be nourishing and cherishing toward the wife. There is such a anointing in the union of marriage. If couples are able to just step back in the midst of the battle and acknowledge what two are able to do in the kingdom. When there are two agreeing on anything, that thing shall be granted. The Word says that a three-fold cord is not easily broken. Now indulge me for a moment. Find a piece of twine or string, now break it. Ok, now get two pieces of string and break it. I'm sure it took a little more strength. Now take three pieces of the same twine and break it. You may or may not have broken it, but I'm sure that you noticed that it wasn't as easy as the one piece. Once marriage is intertwined with the purpose and direction of God it, can't easily break. Somewhere along the line I separated myself from that bond.

After my bishop asked me that very important question instead of truly meditating on it, I had decided that I had already made up my mind. My decision was to forfeit my covering and I told my husband it was over. Unknowing to my husband, my eyes began to sway. I was convinced that my husband had been unfaithful so I was entitled to do the same thing right? Wrong!

I met a man I thought shared the same interests that I had. In my eyesight, he was perfect, better said the wrapping was. It's amazing how exactly when I was broken and distraught from out of nowhere comes perfection! In walks 6 foot dose of a perfect chocolate specimen with the smile I craved. He was an artist. Nothing was more beautiful to me than someone who had learned to express himself in writing, poetry or even music. He listened to my gripes and complaints. I, too, agreed that our spouses were idiots for not seeing the jewels that we were.

Briefly, I want to talk about adultery. People who commit adultery are selfish individuals. Every time we talked, it was this is how I feel. I felt that how I was done wrong, how I felt unfulfilled, and never once had taken responsibility for our own actions in the marriage. After painting the picture of our spouse's infractions and discrepancies, then we paint the image of our own perfection. Don't be tricked! It will never work out. Now, I know there are couples that may read this and say, well mine did… I question you with this when your spouse left the house and didn't tell you where he was going or if you saw him mysteriously hugging someone else you didn't know, did you get a twinge of jealousy? If you did, then that is your seed growing. Every time you think, what if or may be, he could have? It is a reminder that your indiscretion forged a bond that could eventually be severed from another woman's disdain or respect for your marriage. Don't think that just because he chose you or she chose you means that you are now exempt from a repeat performance of infidelity. It takes an extreme amount of forgiveness and prayer to recover from a partner's infidelity. Don't let it tear your marriage apart. If it can be repaired, repair it. But, be honest if it is repeated offenses, then the person may need to be counseled and given time. Communication is key. Never be afraid to ask your spouse what they need. We are not mind readers. As they say it we have two ears and one mouth, so we can listen twice as much as we talk. Ok here's the scripture reference you Bible scholars! *James 1:19-20* says, *"Wherefore, my beloved brethren, let every man be swift to hear, slow to speak, slow to wrath."*

Listening to your spouse may be the key to healing in your marriage and deliverance from the thoughts of infidelity. This man seemed to fill all the gaps I had with my relationship with my husband. When I was married, although I wasn't a virgin, I hadn't experienced many men and this man introduced me to something different. He placed his fingerprint (what is a fingerprint? I'm glad you asked keep reading for the definition) on me intimately. It was hard to remove. He listened to what I was going through and amazing enough he was going through a similar situation. I was so wrapped up in the sin that the Lord himself had to snatch me out. Remember that no matter how deep you get into sin, God always makes a way of escape but understand it wasn't God tempting me or testing me! The Bible says in *James 1:13-14, "Let no man say that when he is tempted I am tempted of God: For God cannot be tempted. But every man is tempted when he is drawn away of his own lust, and enticed."*

The scripture goes on to describe that when temptation is created that it brings sin and with sin comes death. Now some interpret that as physical death and it could be, but I interpret that as spiritual death. I knew that I had not only destroyed my marriage, but the voice of God was almost nonexistent to me. Sin had allowed me to even quiet my conscience as things that normally would have made me feel bad didn't bother me as much. I had given myself over to the last of my flesh and defrauded my marriage.

I was so far gone that my bishop during his own sickness had to leave his bed and drive to my job to tell me that the Lord was unpleased and I needed to get my life right. How grateful I am for his interceding on my behalf. My only excuse was he did it so why can't I," the same excuse that my four-year-old says when her sister snatches a toy from her hand and she snatches it back.

First Corinthians 13:11 says, "When I was a child I spake as a child I understood as a child, I thought as a child: But when I became a man I put away childish things"

When I made the decision to be a wife, I made the decision to abandon childhood antics and games. This is a great time to examine the ways in your own marriage that perhaps you may have acted outside of the way you should have and in the process may have lost a level of trust and communication with your spouse. If you're not married, but in a relationship headed toward marriage these are great opportunities to stand back and think of better ways to communicate with you current significant other. There is nothing worse than carrying baggage, which you didn't even know was there into a marriage, because instead of dealing with the issues you swept it under the rug.

Needless to say, after my fall I saw only glimpses into my mistake and the consequences of my actions. My guilt drove me to confess to my husband as a reason for divorce. He was devastated to say the least. I remember the tears welling in his eyes as he looked at me and said how could you? All I remember is thinking how he dare judge me after his own indiscretion. I realized why after I talked to other men. They told me when a man cheats he's able to do it with little or no emotional attachment, but a woman emotionally decides when and how she cheats. It always starts internally before it's done. I guess that's true because it was very hard to let the affair go, but for the sake of my children I decided that my family was worth more than this kind of happiness.

We knew we needed a get-away, my husband and I decided that we would go on a second honeymoon after four years to this beautiful romantic castle. There, while we watched the sun go down, we confessed our true love to one another. We never had a wedding ceremony, but that night we said the vows that were in our heart. I told him that without him my life was meaningless and he truly taught me how to love. For the first time he was able to say that he needed me. For so long I had longed to know that he needed me, finally with tears streaming down his face he let go and let me in—into the past years disappointment and anger he felt. It was one of the most beautiful moments in our marriage, one I will not forget. If only we didn't have to go back to reality.

Before I go on, I want to tell you tomorrow is not promised to any of us and if there is a special someone in your life that on the dark days brings the sun and on the dark night brings the fire, you make sure they know. Wives sometimes spend so much time complaining that we forget to celebrate what we have. Today make the first thing on your honey-do list be to kiss him senseless and in whatever special way you two share give him the best of you. We wait till we're on husband number two to appreciate what we have after we've torn husband number one to shreds. Real commitment and love are rare and they should be treated as such. One of the things that really stood out to me was when I was in the last counseling session before our divorce. David was living with a woman and I was dating. My bishop said to us, "No one will ever do to each other what you two do to each other." I knew he didn't just mean in the physical sense but the emotional sense. We agreed and he said, "Then why are you getting a divorce?"

David said, "She treats me like I am the best man in the world." There was nothing I could say because he was right. I treated him like he was nothing and she treated him like he was a king. Sometimes we walk around with our spouses thinking that we have him because he can't keep his hands off us but actually I learned this if you think you have gold then there is definitely platinum out there and even if you've got platinum, a man will settle for silver if she treats him right.

Girlfriend Note: ───────────────────────

We are not built with the innate knowledge of the things our mates needs or requires (even though we think so) but with prayer and communication can become experts! Take time to study your man today.

I think that before we even arrived back at our home, we began to argue again. My husband demanded that I never speak to the man ever again. Resorting back to the woman he hated, I lunged accusations at him of infidelity. Our union together became a bunch of strained hellos and grateful goodbyes. After only a few short months, I decided that I didn't want to try anymore. I was tired of the yells and fights. Our home had become a battleground not only in the spiritual sense but in the physical sense. Holes in our walls, pictures of our life ripped apart. My husband now occupied the bedroom and I slept on the couch on the living room. He had even changed the locks in our bedroom so that I wouldn't be able to get in. I assume during this time he was seeing someone, but I will never know.

Our last try was when he told me to come home early and he would cook dinner for us. On the way home I got the urge to call the other man, so I did. It was a quick conversation just how he was doing and how I was as well, but my lapse in judgment cost me my marriage and was the final straw to break the small rope that held us together. My husband had planned a wonderful dinner steak and potatoes with a bottle of wine chilled. We ate mostly in silence and I thought my heart had already left him and the scars we had given each other were becoming more and more visible. I was looking across the table at my enemy and not my lover.

"So David have you thought about the separation?" I asked looking down not wanting to see his eyes.

"I mean Nadia I was hoping that we could try to work this out and get along," David responded.

"I don't think so David. I desperately want to see how to live by myself and learn how to take care of myself. I'm tired of fighting you and living in this mess" Frustrated from his lack of realization that this marriage was over.

"Would you like a glass of wine? I've almost finished the bottle," David said. I was becoming visibly annoyed at his avoidance of the subject at hand.

"Look David, I'm not interested in anything to drink, you don't even drink so why are you doing it now. Look let's just talk about it later. Dinner's great you're getting really good at cooking I'm sure the restaurant will be great." Trying my best to be civil during the difficult situation I just looked across the table and I asked myself what I must have been thinking to get married at such a young age before I even knew myself. Here I was trapped in a marriage with a man that I couldn't stand and barely tolerated. We had grown so far apart that after my miscarriage a few months ago we didn't even mourn. We were more grateful that out of this broken mess we were calling a marriage we hadn't produced any more children. We were in the worst financial state that we had ever been. I didn't even know the half. In six years we had lost a house, a baby, our trust of one another and had countless scars not just physically, but emotionally. All I could think was whatever you do God, get me out of here dead or alive.

"So Nadia why don't we sit down and talk?" David asked slyly inviting me to join him in the living room on the floor. Honestly, I was gagging on the inside not because my husband repelled me, I was just not anxious to enjoy such close proximity time with him.

"Sure no problem David, but I was extremely tired so let's be quick," I said dragging myself away from the table and into the adjoining living room. Before I knew it David and I were doing something that was similar to making love but not being very successful at it. It was all routine and so uninteresting that I imagine David made himself enjoy it just so he could be finished. That was the moment we both knew what we didn't want to say that after six years of marriage and three beautiful children, that the only thing we ever got right was over and with it went the loyalty. As I retreated to clean up, I sent a text to the other man, leaving my phone in the restroom. My husband became suspicious of the sudden change in my behavior, leaving the phone in the restroom was not my norm so he got up and went to see why I left it. The other man had sent a message back and David saw the text. This started a world war in the house. With fear of exposing him (love covers), I will say that our argument was tremendous and resulted in me looking for an apartment the next day. He apologized and told me that he would leave the house and allow me some space but he didn't want me to go. I told him that I thought it was best, especially after some unfortunate encounters with his temper he agreed.

Uncovered, Uncontrolled, Unhappy

When I left my husband and moved into my apartment, I was lost to say the least. I had begun dating a man that I found out later had a live-in girlfriend. I had lost my job where I just had received a promotion and now I was working in a local bar to make money. We will call this the wilderness in life.

I want you to see what happens when you don't know who you are in God, lose sight of your calling and move before the Lord tells you to. I was still very much in love with my husband and I think I did everything I could to cover my pain in every addiction I could get my hands on. I thought so little of myself that I even resorted to sharing a man just to have one. One major thing I learned was that even if he does leave her, why would you want his cheating tail? The Word says that you are fearfully and wonderfully made you deserve to be treated like the beautiful woman you are. When you are in a state of separation, it's not time to party, but time to reflect on how to be healed from the impending divorce, if there is no way to reconcile. After seeing that I had made a mistake in wanting a divorce, I went to David and asked him if we could work it out and be a family, but he declined. David had moved on, dating a woman that he had met in the last phase of our separation. That didn't stop us from being intimate, although it was shallow and impassionate but familiar.

I comforted myself with the thought that if I couldn't have all of him I'd make sure that the other woman wasn't getting his all either. Shameful how I allowed myself to be a pawn in the enemy's plan to not only destroy him but me in the process. David was God's chosen vessel, living the way that was not pleasing God. More importantly it was not the behavior of two people that God had called early in life to live for Him.

The woman he was with gave him everything he wanted. Watching her have the man I forfeited was rough. I can remember some moments when I was crying and in emotional pain I'd call David and ask him for help and he'd tell me that this is what I wanted. He was right! As a result of abandoning my covering unequipped, I was financially struggling. My lights were constantly off and bills were overwhelming me. Thanks to my bad budgeting, things were only getting worse. Now if the married care for the things of the world and the single cares for the things of the Lord, then after my divorce I should have been focusing on redeveloping my desires for Christ. Instead I searched for a bed replacement that could eventually become my happily-ever-after. I can't stress enough how important it is during our single life to learn truly who Christ is. Developing a relationship with Christ who the Bible calls our first love in

Revelations 2:3 is the only way to experience our true identity. It is very easy to "know" a man after their flesh romantically, but the Lord desires to "know" us in our fears, triumphs and dreams.

I challenge you before I go on with this thought "He that findeth a wife…"

If we haven't learned to care for the things of the Lord, how can we be effective wives to a potential husband. The closer we get to Christ, the more he reveals about our character, both the good and bad traits. When we continually engage in relationships with new people we become distracted and miss precious intimate time with Christ. In essence we lose sight of who we are trying to become suitable for the man or woman courting us. I'm not saying that I believe that dating is wrong, I just believe that we must evaluate our reasoning for wanting to be in the relationship.

Girlfriend Note: ────────────────────────

> *To all my beautiful single sanctified sistas, Don't Settle Wait on God! He is not the only one who will love you, If he doesn't treasure you then let him go, Don't chase him it says " He that findeth...."*
>
> *YOU ARE FEARFULLY AND WONDERFULLY MADE BEAUTIFUL ON THE OUTSIDE AND INSIDE AND YOU DESERVE SOMEONE WHO WILL CONFIRM WHAT GOD HAS ALREADY TOLD YOU. Time is not running out so stop looking at your watch.*

I want to be as transparent about my own experiences as I can. This transparency requires me to talk about divorce because it was unfortunately my reality.

Divorce felt like an unwelcome 7.5 category hurricane ripping through my life leaving no survivors. The reality of divorce is worse than the act. Even after the paper is signed and the gavel dropped, it still wasn't real for me. I know that I had originally been the one that asked for the divorce, but it was based from the pain and emotion I was feeling. We continued to cling to one another intimately even after I left. So I thought even though his mouth said we were over, I had convinced myself that because we were physically attached that his heart was still with me. The reality, which I found out later, was that our connection was 90 percent physical. The reality, albeit harsh, is that although we were physically compatible, emotionally we couldn't be more incompatible. I would often pass by the men's department and see shirts my ex liked and almost bought them even after the separation. It was very difficult to come to terms that we would no longer be together. If I said that losing him was like losing a part of myself, it would be an understatement. You must allow yourself to mourn. The next hardest thing to handle is the reality that I would lose several friends.

David and I had mutual friends who were now forced to choose sides, because we had both confided very personal things about our marriage. Another huge regret I have is inviting the voice of other people inside our marriage.

There are two harsh lessons that I learned from divorce that I want to share with you.

1. Marriage is a relationship between two people. This seems obvious, but how often do we share personal details about our spouses with "girl-friends" under the pretense that I was getting advice. The Word speaks clearly about this subject in *Genesis 2:23 "Therefore shall a man leave his father and mother; and shall join with his wife; and they shall be one flesh."*

It also is very clear about what we confess to others not because the Lord wants us to be secretive but because he wants the warring to be done on our face for our spouses not with our tongue. The Word says in *James 5:16, "Confess your faults one to another, and pray for one another, that ye may be healed. The fervent effectual prayers of the righteous availeth much."*

The small mistakes can cause a huge gap of division in a marriage and can also cause a lack of trust.

My purpose in revealing our shortcomings became an avenue or outlet to dump my reasons of why I thought my husband was not functioning in his role and a way to show that I was better than he. I began to want to be like my single friends who constantly told me how great life was. They had accomplished all these things and I felt like I was missing something.

If you receive nothing from this book, please take this "keep what happens in your home between you and your spouse! Unless there is violence involved, of course." The Lord created Godly counsel for those other areas that are lacking, Make an appointment with whoever is assigned in your local church body to handle marriage counseling. Don't go spreading around your issues because those things can hinder another person in the ministry especially if after you two have restored your marriage now your spouse has to minister to them.

Sorry, mini detour!!!!

2. When you're going through a divorce it's important to allow yourself to go through the steps in order to heal and come out of it healthy. It's not an overnight process and if you try to stick it in the microwave, you will only come out either overdone or underdone.

I was more wounded from the denial I self-inflicted about how I felt about David than anything. I convinced myself that I didn't want to be tied down so I was determined to get what I needed from a man and discard them.

It wasn't until after I was terribly damaged and hurt that I realized what an adverse affect this theory would have on my life. I went from guy to guy searching for something I believed the other had been lacking. Ultimately, what I thought my ex husband was lacking, I never found. I never dealt with the ways I had contributed to my marriage's shortcomings or the defects I had personally that led to our divorce. But the worse part about it is that I hadn't allowed myself the time to get to know who I was as a single adult. I only knew the position of wife and mother for so long that to be anyone else felt impossible.

I didn't know how to make it financially and hadn't learned how valuable it was to just embrace singleness and being in the presence of the Lord and his people as much as possible. So my mind thought that I should have a man but I knew that I only wanted the physical part of a relationship. I wasn't ready to attach myself emotionally to someone because as wounded as I was, eventually I would end up hurting myself and wasting their time.

Imagine for a moment that you have a broken leg and the more that you try to self-treat the broken leg, the worse it gets. Over time as the leg goes untreated and you continue to walk on it, it develops an infection and the healing process takes longer that it would have if you would have just gone to the hospital from the beginning! You go to the hospital but too little too late, as now they are forced to amputate the leg because of your own stubbornness to get help! This analogy although dramatic correctly depicts what we do when we don't take time to allow God to finish healing us from the hurts of our past.

I can't stress enough how important it is to seek help! Don't just try to cover your pain with the world's system of pain relievers. They will only give you a temporary fix. Once the sun comes up and the migraines develop, the problem and pain will still be there. Trust me I tried to cover my pain in the comfort of a man. Besides a broken heart more times than once, I should have chosen to seek after righteousness rather than a bedmate! In *Isaiah 61:1-3* says, *"The Spirit of the Lord GOD [is] upon me; because the LORD hath anointed me to preach good tidings unto the meek; he hath sent me to bind up the brokenhearted, to proclaim liberty to the captives, and the opening of the prison to [them that are] bound; 61:2 To proclaim the acceptable year of the LORD, and the day of vengeance of our God; to comfort all that mourn;"*

It goes on to say in *61:3, "To appoint unto them that mourn in Zion, to give unto them beauty for ashes, the oil of joy for mourning, the garment of praise for the spirit of heaviness; that they might be called trees of righteousness, the planting of the LORD, that he might be glorified"*

The Lord wants to heal us from the destruction and devastation divorce causes but it's up to us to accept His help. I heard a popular Nashville Pastor in Nashville say during a conference say that "the more that we try to handle on our own the more that God puts on us to show us that we can't handle it at all" How true the Lord wants to fix what has been broken, but it's up to us to come before the throne as empty as we have felt, without pride about how we were wronged but with the pain that no one sees and lay it at His feet. I can't tell you how the Lord is healing me everyday thanks to my own surrender.

If you've felt this emptiness pray this prayer with me:

Dear Heavenly Father, I thank you right now for my life. I thank you that you love me in spite of how I've acted in the past. I bless you for forgiving any thought or action that is not like you. I come to you acknowledging the pain and emptiness that divorce has left me feeling. I acknowledge that I am unable to handle this pain I'm feeling alone. I thank You that

Your Word says that I should cast my cares upon You because You care for me. I know that in spite of all of this that you will get the glory from my life. That all things are working together for my good. God, put in me right now the spirit of forgiveness. Forgiveness for anyone I have felt that transgressed against me and teach me how to forgive myself. I know that your blood has covered every sin and every thought that is not like you. I praise you right now for the spirit of joy that falls on me now as I release this over to You.

In Jesus name,

Amen.

COMMERCIAL BREAK: CHRISTIAN DATING

As I began to study, several things came to me on dating and also several references. The Bible reveals how this should take place. One of the first things I realized is that whatever the world tells you in regard to dating is WRONG!

If the idea is not backed up with righteous doctrine, it is false. I don't care if your girlfriend tells you that you can convert him, it's a trick from the pit. If a man comes into your path and doesn't know God, then your responsibility is to win him to Christ not win him with your kisses. Show him to God not, if he comes to God he gets you. If the basis for your relationship is built as you being the prize, the minute you make him angry he relates the emotions he feels for you as a reason not to seek God for himself. Think of how many times the Lord has brought someone to us and we become more concerned with what he looked like than if his soul was secure in heaven. After he's been saved and has begun his path to God, if it's God's will for you two to begin a relationship, the foundation has been laid and will not be compromised with condemnation. Listed below are some things I found in my study.

A. Before considering a mate I think it's necessary to make a self-evaluation.

Ask yourself what your motive is for wanting a mate in your life?

Our purpose in the earth is to glorify Him and continue in the endeavor He came and died for. We should continue as disciples *"compelling them to come in, that my house be filled," Luke 14:23.* We should be increasing the kingdom's souls and not just interested in what can please our flesh. The Word also goes on to say that we should not be careful or anxious for nothing, but in every circumstance and in everything, by prayer and petition *Philippians 4:6* (definite request), with thanksgiving, continue to make your wants known to God (*Philippians 4:6 Amplified*). God already knows the plan He has for us and whatever is lacking in your life, He will and can provide.

Is your life in order for the Lord to send that man of God?

The Word states that *"a man that findeth a good thing and obtains favour in the Lord," says Proverbs 18:22.* Now ask yourself, "Are you really a good thing?" Before we address that, I want you to meditate on the word wife. I asked myself why use this instead of mate? Because the unmarried woman cares for the things of the Lord and in essence she is married to the Lord, according to *First Corinthians 7:34.* How can you be the wife of the Lord if you're more concerned with how to find someone tangible to satisfy some fleshy desire? One can't serve two masters because he will hate one or the other, *Luke 16:13.* Anything that consumes your constant thought rules over you that include watching for a wedding ring every time you meet a man. I speak from experience. I read this theory in action in Ruth. She was gleaning in the field, I believe translated for us we are working in the ministry that our Boaz will see us and inquire who we are.

B. The other area is if we know how to tend our own home and have self control in our finances. When God created Eve and brought her to Adam he told her that she would be a Help mate, *Genesis 2:18*. That means exactly as it says meet the man of God with help not hurt. Are your finances so out of control you're looking for a savior on a white horse, or is your home unkempt and unmaintained? Do you spend more time in the drive-thru than the kitchen? If these areas need to be improved the Word even tells us that we can seek the help of our elder women in the body to help us learn, *Titus 2:4*.

Another self-evaluation: how do you feel about yourself?

Are you looking for someone to help you validate who you think you are? When was the last time that you did something for yourself in the area of pampering? Although it's cliché, aside from Christ no one will love you as good and as much as you will, And if you've been through several unhealthy relationships with men, then it might be safe to say that you may need to get back to the basics of just loving you. Taking a few extra moments to care for how you look on the outside may give you an extra boost in your esteem. Also reciting the Word of God to reaffirm who you are everyday may also help. *Proverbs 139:14* and *First Peter 2:9* say that you deserve the best. If God gave His very best to you, how much should you give to yourself. One of the things I loved about Ruth is that she was very confident even from the beginning when she told Naomi that her husband died, even knowing that her people were cursed. The chances of Naomi having another son and waiting for him to grow to adulthood were slim she still said, *Ruth 2:2. "Let me now go to the field, and glean ears of corn after him in whose sight I shall find grace..."* She didn't doubt she declared that she would find that grace and favor.

C. Now, if you can answer these questions favorably and God has sent a man into your life that you feel is Boaz, I would still ask some important questions.

In what environment did you meet this person?

How did you begin your relationship? How did you write the beginning, middle and end of your story together? His first impression of you will govern his thoughts of you. The Word says that we should not be unequally yoked, *Second Corinthians, 6:14*, for the greatest reason that darkness can't be associated with light. If the couple doesn't believe in the same things it can cause problem later on as the relationship develops. You'll be more interested in doing things to help the church and the other person won't understand unless the mystery has been revealed.

How will this relationship help advance and strengthen the kingdom?

God acknowledges that there is a power in the unity of two *"....That if two of you shall agree on earth as touching anything that they shall ask it, it shall be done for them of my father which is in heaven."* He even says in *Deuteronomy 32:30, "...one chase a thousand, and two put ten thousand to flight..."* There is an awesome anointing in the power of two, if the motive of each party is right. Christ left us with the assignment to teach all the nations the things that he has commanded. Your union should be created to use that power given by the Holy Spirit to be greater soul winners in the Kingdom.

Have you sought Christian counsel concerning your union?

"Where no counsel is, the people fall..." Proverbs 11:14. God has sent a Sheppard over our souls and before we make any decisions we should consult the man and woman of God for they answer to God for your souls. Even before Boaz married Ruth he had to speak to a group of elders and he received counsel concerning their union. Sometimes we become so wrapped up in our emotions, which change daily, that we can't see clearly. So God placed a Word concerning relationships in our leaders. He calls for us to be wise as serpents but harmless as doves so that we don't fall into a trap. After we've been given

the specific instructions on how to continue and have successfully completed them, then we'll be given the blessings of God. Then, if it's ordained by God, it should be given prosperity blessings. *"May the Lord make the woman who is coming into your house like Rachel and Leah, the two who built the household of Israel? May you do worthily and get wealth (power) in Ephratah, and be famous in Bethlehem," Ruth 4:11 Amplified Bible.*

I pray that this is a blessing to you as much as it was for me to write. I found myself lacking in a few areas that I needed to improve if I wanted the Lord to send my Boaz.

Back to the story...

The Word of God is clear that sin separates us from God so while I was out being disobedient He couldn't save me. God is a gentle God in terms of ushering us to him. He won't beg and plead with us to do what's best for us. *Revelations 3:20* says, *"Behold, I stand at the door, and knock: if any man hears my voice, and opens the door, I will come in to him, and will sup with him and he with me."*

While I was consuming myself in sin, He was there waiting for me to return to my first love, the One that loved me before there was ever a David and Nadia. The one that wiped my tears when I felt rejected about being adopted or when I was sexually assaulted by a strange man. He was the same God that brought my sisters to me and showed me through my parents that just because some doctor said I would have a learning disability, doesn't mean that they or I had to accept that fate. I began to look at the world's view of how I should live and began to do things that were harmful to my body and even more harmful to my spirit. The voice of God seemed further and further away. I asked myself, "Where are the church friends I thought I had." I knew that I was doing wrong, but I can remember just one of them calling to chastise me, thanks Ora Brown. She saw me in the mess of the wilderness and she walked up to me and gave me a much needed Word of encouragement and also rebuke. Sometimes we don't just need that gentle hug, sometimes hearing that God is unpleased with our behavior and disregard of His commandments is needed too. I am extremely indebted to her for her obedience to God that Sunday. I know now that God wanted me to seek Him out. It was like the Lord was calling me and I was running in the other direction. One of the reasons I ran was because I felt like a failure. I had failed as a daughter, a mother, a wife and worse of all as a woman of God. The Lord was whispering that He would make the ashes of my soul beautiful, but I only heard the negative words that surrounded me and caused me to hide in shame. I know this is a far cry from the young lady that wanted to save the world's young people. Now, it was all I could do to try to find God once more. It was better to accept the fate of having someone else's man than waiting for God to heal me and send a man of God into my life. I went from man to man searching for pieces of who I was. Along the way I was picking up soul ties and fingerprints.

Fingerprints 8

When one thinks of a fingerprint, they think about something that is used in criminal cases to find the bad guy. Webster's Dictionary defines fingerprints as any identifying characteristic. Did you know every time a man that is not your husband touches you he leaves a finger print on your body? A little piece of himself or his identity and you become a part of him. The more fingerprints tarnish your body, the more of your identity you lose. We've all heard that fornication is the only sin that is against a man's own body.

WOW!

Mr. Fingers left the evidence that he's left his seed inside you. I warn you that though a condom can protect you from disease, it can't protect you from the spirits that he's left lingering. No matter how many times you scrub your body, his fingerprints are still there. That's why sometimes you can't sleep at night because of the dreams that you have after you've laid with a man. Or, did you ever think of the last time you were intimate with someone and visions of the another man came into your mind. That's because you still have his identifying marks over your body.

Let's talk about the very sensitive topic of touch. The fingerprints are the after effect of a single touch. There were several times in the Bible where God told individuals not to touch something. When they touched something that may be cursed or forbidden, it was given the permission to inhabit or affect their life in a negative way. When someone disobeyed that commandment there were sore repercussions. In the New Testament, Christ was amongst the multitude and along came someone sick with an issue of blood and she'd been everywhere, to every doctor. She said if "I can just touch the hem of His garment, then I can be made whole." Amongst the huge crowd, Jesus felt someone touch the hem of His garment and knew that a piece of His virtue was gone. When someone touches one of God's anointed holy vessels it's as if a piece of their virtue leaves. We have to protect the Holy Spirit that lives on the inside of us. God desired but for one to touch you and that was the one he joined you with in marriage. We've been going around from man to man, woman to woman, allowing them to put their identifying marks on us and we wonder why it's so hard to find the right one. It's because it's almost impossible to see you with all marks covering your body.

Now let's talk about what makes up a fingerprint because it's imperative to know how such a tiny thing has solved millions of murders and cases in science. It is because with every fingerprint there is a distinguishing line that is different from anyone else in the world. They are no fingerprints the same. They may have similar curves but are different. When someone touches your body that you aren't in covenant with (marriage), then they leave something on you. Maybe they leave homosexuality, maybe drug abuse, maybe hostility and rage. You never know until after the act is over. We think that a shower can take the smudges away, but as the Bible says what is done in the dark shall come to light. So everyone doesn't know your business, but all of a sudden you find yourself struggling in an area that you've never had problems with before. It's because the fingerprint is still there. Look at the woman of Samaria sitting at the well, *John 4:4-18*. She was conversing with Jesus, and He told her to go back and bring her husband to drink. She replied that she wasn't married. She had the fingerprints from someone and He could see them. He went on to tell this woman that she had been with five men and none of them were her husband either.

Ouch, that's a lot of fingerprints. The only way to remove these fingerprints is to ask the Lord to forgive you and truly turn and allow the blood of Jesus to cover this sin. Trust me He can. His blood will cover every blotch and every scar that has been placed on your body.

Now, I want to talk to those of you that may have had fingerprints placed on your body without your consent through molestation or rape. First, recognize that the actions of another person were not your fault. Nothing you said and nothing you wore gave anyone permission to touch you without your consent. You can't walk around with that pain anymore. You can't keep blaming yourself and your circumstance. You didn't deserve that. Molestation can minimize your personal perceived value of your body. Your body is priceless and God loves you. He will never leave you or forsake you. You have to accept His love first and know that God was there and he loves you.

Next, you have to know that your body is vessel of glory and God has a significant plan just for you. Don't neglect your healing any more. You can't keep walking around like superwoman or superman acting as if what they did to you was nothing. It was not little or minute and yes it was heartless and cruel. You have to be healed and if you haven't forgiven yourself and that person who wronged you, then you must. Forgiveness will free you and talking about what happened to you will release the secret. Secrets of that magnitude can hold you hostage because of their shame, but opening up the wound, although painful, can give it the proper time for repair. God desires the fingerprints to no longer cover your body, so He made it that the blood and love of Jesus would replace the tarnishes.

I remember a particular incident that showed me that it was time to gather my personal wits and get my life together. I decided to go back to my church, as hard as it was. By now David had married. He and his wife not only attended the church where we had first met, but were also operating in the ministry that David and I had worked in. I was sitting in the back. The visiting preacher was preaching. She was describing the wild and reckless behavior that her daughter was displaying. In her wisdom she told her that if she continued, she would no doubt "slip and tip up on something."

Sure enough, the daughter, came home distraught telling her mother of a little package that would be joining their lives in eight or nine months. Oh, I thought that was the funniest thing! I remember being one of the ones laughing out loud. Later that week I woke up with the usual sickness the day before my period and knew that my cycle would follow. Well blah, blah, blah you know the rest. My fate read back to me on a little blue stick and double lines. I took two because surely I couldn't be pregnant. Well I was, I didn't know who the father was? I was jacked up and tore up on the outside and the inside. I had been with a few men and although they were men that I was very close with I had been irresponsible. Where could I go now? The truth was that as a result of my behavior a little life was coming. I was devastated. I ran to my mother and she couldn't help me. I ran to my friends who could only offer me the suggestion of the unthinkable. Here's my disclaimer: First of all fornication is the only sin that is against your own body!

First Corinthians 6:18 says that further more our bodies as a single individual belong solely to the Lord! Besides the sin I brought directly to my body, I also had to reap says *Galatians 6:7*. The reaping came in the way of emotional roller coasters. Outside of the train wreck my life was in, I had grieved the

Holy Spirit and this was a direct result of me not yielding to God in every area of my life.

My first reaction was to do what all my friends told me. Even now when I think of it I almost weep. How dare I even consider doing something so horrible to an innocent life that didn't ask to be here? The fact that I was having unprotected sex was completely my fault and I had to take responsibility for it. My life continued slipping further away until I had even began to slip into a deep depression. Not only had I surrendered my marriage, I was moving further away from the person who God had called me to be. I hated myself and when I looked in the mirror I couldn't believe that my life had turned so quickly in another direction. My girlfriend, Jewel, often says that she had to learn her worth. Unfortunately at this place in my life I had no idea who in the world I was. I woke up one morning and realized that I could no longer live this life. I had two beautiful little girls that loved their mommy. I know they knew under the sheet that mommy put on that she was very unhappy. I would crawl in my bed at night and cry burning tears into my pillow. I couldn't blame anyone but myself. I opened the night stand and pulled out a bunch of letters that my ex had written when we met. How we claimed our love for one another with scripture *First John 4:18* says, *"There is no fear in love but perfect love casteth out fear."* I found all the cards I had kept and held them close against my heart because I remembered that was the last time I had truly felt happy with him. I had been driving past this church and I had decided that I couldn't wait any longer. It was time for me to take that step into my destiny. I couldn't keep holding on to the regret of my marriage and no longer hold on the mistakes of my past. It was time to come from underneath the gutter and rock that I had allowed myself to crawl under. I attended Crusade Dominion Church. After the pastor was preaching, she said that God had led her to pray for people that had been holding on to something for years. God said it was time to let it go. I watched person after person go running to the line giving over the baggage that weighed them down. She continued praying and explaining in detail the things God would deliver them from. With a pronounced tone she went up and down the line. She just couldn't stop asking for people. Then finally she said, "There's someone else, you've even made a shrine for this person or this thing that you've held onto for years."

Tears streaming down my face, I remembered that morning waking up from a sad night wiping my eyes and stepping on the pictures of David and me and going into my day. I knew instantly that the Lord was calling me and I had to answer. I went up in the line. She said she knew it was me. That was the day that I will never forget. I gave my heart to God and I haven't turned back. A few short weeks later as I was evaluating my life, I began to redevelop my relationship with God. I told him that I wanted to move out of Atlanta. I wanted an opportunity to start over and find out whom Nadia was. I wanted an opportunity to learn who I really was without the pain of my past slapping me in my face every day. I wrote a letter to my former bishop and pastor telling them of my decision and how much I loved them.

I called my ex-aunt and I asked her about the cost of living in Nashville and she told me and I began to go on the prayer rampage. I knew that in order for my prayers to be answered I had to line all areas of my life back up with God. Sin separates us from God, it prevents his hear from hearing us. The Word speaks of this in *Isaiah 59:1 and 2, "Behold, the Lord's hand is not shortened, that it cannot save; neither His ear heavy, that it cannot hear: But your iniquities have separated between you and your God, and your sins have hid His face from you, that He will not hear."*

God wants to bless us but he can't reach past our sin to do it. I knew I had to truly give up those things that were keeping my prayers hindered.

Can a girl say "no"…?

The dilemma in front of me was that I was in deep like with a man that could possibly not be the father of the child I was carrying and certainly not the "Jesus" type. We were still intimate and unmarried. Yet I was begging God to help me get my life in order. I kept wondering why I was receiving no answer. Finally I heard the Word it's time to live Holy. Holy means to be set apart not separated but there should be a clear vision that I was called of God. How could I continue to claim Jesus when I was denying his power every time I gave into my flesh? How could I tell someone that God can deliver if I didn't know that delivering power for myself? I started trying to fight my flesh on my own, telling myself that if I was in that situation I could say no.

Well I couldn't. Suddenly it dawned on me that this was a battle I could not fight alone. I realized that I had been going about the fighting of my flesh the wrong way. Whenever we begin to lose our way, it's best to start at the beginning and examine the map more carefully. In *Galatians 2:20*, it says, *"I am crucified with Christ: nevertheless I live; yet not I, but Christ liveth in me: and the life which I now live in the flesh I live by the faith of the Son of God, who loved me, and gave Himself for me."*

That means that my life is lead by God because I am in constant reliance and trust in Him. The reason it was so hard to submit to His purpose and flee from my flesh was two things:

1. It was uncommon and uncomfortable to let go of the need to want to be with a man physically. I craved the physical gratification fornication brought to me.

2. I just didn't want to stop.

The Word says that if we submit to God and resist the devil, he would flee. Well, I never really resisted. I allowed myself to go into situations well aware of the outcome but because I was waiting for this divine being to fly from the sky and stop me from sin, I didn't stop. God has given us free will; He created sex so he was well aware of the pleasure involved. Just like so many other things in life, we have perverted its original intentions and turned it into something ugly. God intended sex for marriage, not one day before. He is unpleased with the callous and uncaring way I had regarded it and used it for my own selfish pleasure and desire. God wants to cleanse us of every unhealthy desire and give us the greater desires, but we must submit to Him and allow Him to change us from the inside out.

The first thing I had to do was to watch my eye gate. I could no longer watch movies that sent my imagination to Jupiter. I couldn't go certain places that would remind me of the life I was giving up. I quit my job at the club. We don't realize that a lot of our motivations or actions greatly are influenced by what we see.

In *First John 2:16*, it says, *"For all that is in the world, the lust of the flesh, and the lust of the eyes, and the pride of life, is not of the Father, but is of the world."*

The world is full of pretty painted pictures we can have if we submit to what looks good. But the Word tells what we see can contribute to the selfish lust in our lives. Not just physical feelings, but also in the area of what we feel we must obtain such as materialistic desires.

Starting Over 9

The most extreme change in my life was that I decided to move. I was seven months pregnant and I went into some serious prayer about this decision. It was time to search the scriptures again and petition heaven for the direction He wanted me to take about the move. I began writing everything down and backing up the things I wanted with the Word of God. I knew that number one, my motives had to be right. Was I running from my destiny or did I really desire to start a fresh? Where would I move? My beautiful daughters still needed their father and Laila is convinced that grandma is the greatest being on the earth. Where would I work if I left the city? Could I transfer? So here were the prayers or petitions to God.

> *Lord, You said in Your Word that if any man lack wisdom, we should ask You who gives it liberally, James 1:5 and God I also know that if I would delight myself in Your Word, that You would give me the desires of my heart. Psalms 37:1. God, my desires aren't selfish. I seek to do the will of God free of the condemnation that I have placed upon myself with my own mistakes. Lord, I know that You have come that I may have life*

and liberty. John 10:10 You don't desire for Your chosen generation, First
Peter 2:9and 5:7, to be burdened by their thoughts and lifestyle you ask
us to cast our cares unto you because you care for us. I leave this at Your
alter and I wait patiently for You to answer in the way of confirmation.
I love You and in advance praise You for answering my prayer.

I have to tell you that my decision came with its own disappointment to my Mother and Father. They were more concerned with the well being of their grandchildren. I was just learning how to budget and take care of myself. I was moving far away from them. After I really prayed, then came the research the Word says that faith without works is dead, *James 2:17*. So I started inquiring. At the time David's Aunt and I had regained contact. She told me that she lived in Nashville. I had never lived anywhere else in my life. Nashville seemed close enough. I inquired about the cost of living and she helped me. Not only did she help me find a place to live for my daughters, she was there as a shoulder and voice of reason when I was discouraged in Atlanta. Things were dramatically changing around me, I was making a life changing decision not only pregnant but also with two little girls that could possible not recover mentally from the separation. I have to admit that I was terrified. No one was on my side. Some people were even beginning to place bets on if I would make it two months. All I had was Jesus and the determination that I would finally grab a whole on my life and allow the Lord to heal every wound and self afflicted pain that I had subjected myself to.

Sometimes in life we have to leave our comfort zone and go where the only voice we hear is the Lord's. With the voices of our reality screaming around us, sometimes, it's almost impossible to hear the voice of God clearly. I cared more about the opinion of God than man's opinion. They only knew the Nadia of the past and weren't open to the new one. In *Galatians 1:15-16* it says, *"But when it pleased God, who separated me from my mother's womb, and called me by His grace, To reveal his Son in me, that I might preach Him among the heathen; immediately I conferred not with flesh and blood..."*

The Apostle Paul was recanting that it was God who had called him before the voices of his people ever did. He understood that sometimes in this life you have to be more driven by the plan of God then the plan man has in store for us. We have to be concerned with the Father's business because He tells us that if we seek God first that all things will be added unto us. He knows what we have need of. I promise that He will supply every one if we are in His will and certainly if we're in His purpose.

So after being given permission to leave Atlanta, I set off to Nashville with only a few bumps along the way. I was beginning to see the move of God in every area of my life and His favor seemed to radiate on me like never before.

I had a beautiful baby girl, Audrey Rose, November 26. She has brought a joy into my life that I didn't know I had. I followed through with the things necessary for her well-being and now am comfortable with my decisions. I released the thought of how I believed my life should go, and allowed God to lead me. In the first week of my life-changing move, I found a church home Abundant Life Ministry under the guidance of Pastor Mike and Lady Michelle Whitsey. I was being fed the Word that brings about a real change. I have met the most incredible people since I moved here. Even though I miss my family and friends, Jewel, Dina, Monique, I have never been happier with my life. I won't say that this walk is easy. I promise His Word never says it will be, but what He does promise is that He will never leave you or forsake you.

Christ has been there for me every step of the way. So, if you have been praying and asking God for a change in your life because like me you know you can't go another second without his guidance, pray this prayer with me.

Father in the Name of Jesus, I come to You now repenting of all my sins. The ones I did out loud in front of others and the secret hidden sins that I thought no one saw. I know that You saw them and I repent of grieving You. I know You loved me more than myself. Right now I give You my heart; I no longer want to live in the bondage that sin creates for me. I desire Your will is greater than my own. I desire Your purpose. God guides me in the way that You lead and in the things that please You. Teach me how to walk the walk of faith and teach me how to protect my thoughts from evil. I know that You have given Your life for me and it is through Your blood that I am made whole right now. I thank You in advance for Your love and Your direction.

In Jesus mighty name I pray.

If you've prayed that prayer, I demand now that you forgive yourself...Allow the Lord to heal you and forgive the mistakes of your past. They are your past. *Romans 8:1-2* states, *"there is therefore now no condemnation to them which are in Christ Jesus, who walk not after the flesh, but after the Spirit. For the law of the Spirit of life in Christ Jesus hath made me free from the law of sin and death. God has made you free right now if you believe it."*

I wish that I had some fairy tale ending to tell, but blessed be to The Most Highest that every day He writes my story with His happy ending.

"Now unto him that is able to keep you from falling, and to present you faultless before the presence of his glory with exceeding joy to the only wise God our Savior, be glory and majesty, dominion and power, both now and ever. Amen."

Jude 1:24-25

Epilogue

After I had been working in Nashville for a year, God decided that it was time for me to return to Atlanta. That's just what I did. I moved back in March. After many tears and pain, I decided to find Audrey's father. While I had been trying for quite some time to narrow down my date of conception, I couldn't. So, I called the guy that I had last been with. He was not her father and I was angry, frustrated and devastated. I looked at Audrey and wondered what I was to do.

She was happy and I decided that I could just be mommy and daddy until God sent her one. I decided that I would no longer mourn the mistakes of my past and that if God wanted him found then he would. My friends didn't agree and convinced me to call an old friend that I had been crazy about. We had been together one time since breaking up. He was handsome, charming and had a smile that could melt a girl's heart. After contacting his family, I waited for his call. A few days later I received his call. Once I heard his voice echoing off the other end, my heart skipped a beat. He told me that he wanted to go to dinner to discuss Audrey. I was afraid of him seeing the new improved calmer Nadia so I declined. Eventually, I swallowed hard and agreed to meet him on my birthday, August 13.

I had spent most of the day prepping for my girl's night out with my best friend when he called and asked if I could come over to see him. With nervous chills running all over me I accepted. I was ready for Audrey to know her father but unsure of how I would feel after seeing him after so much time had passed. Before I pulled into his driveway I looked in the mirror and convinced myself that I could do this. I gave myself the verbal affirmation "Nadia, he's just a guy. So what if he's gorgeous. God has delivered you from that mess. Whatever you do don't touch him." Once I had talked myself into opening the car door I got out. I walked around the car and the door slowly opened. The smile that followed, wow! I couldn't get around the car fast enough to hug him. I was eager to find out how he'd been in the two years of our separation. My memories were filled with thoughts of heavy drinking, sex and partying! I was different now. I wasn't about to expose my baby to the life of my past. I was ready for him to say something derogatory because that's the way we interacted. I recalled our last meeting and as unpleasant as it was I walked out of his life tears streaming down my eyes because I was pregnant, and he was more concerned with being a playboy. In the present, he looked different now more lean and muscular with longer locks. I wondered beneath the new look was the same man lurking there? We sat down on the couch and we studied each other. He looked over and said, " So what are you doing for God now?" I was without words. The man that wouldn't go into the church if they were giving away shots of Cognac was asking me about my walk with God.

We began to talk about how the Lord had changed him and how he was now saved and that old life was no more. Skip forward eight months later, Audrey has her father and Boaz found me. March 5, 2010 I said I do to my husband and I haven't stop smiling yet.

Now I won't deceive you into believing that it was an easy road learning to forgive and how to learn to love but God teaches me. I am open and receptive to the Voice of God and also to my husband. You're wondering who stole my husband… the culprit was me. I allowed my ex husband to be taken from me because in the end I spent more time rationalizing how it was biblical to get out of my marriage but never used the Bible to save it.

Stay tuned "How I kept my Husband"

Moral of the story……. Just let God do it because I promise when He works it out it's so much sweeter!

I learned a valuable lesson about marriage one I hope you hear today.

Success in marriage doesn't merely depend on choosing the "right" one but must include *you* being the "right" one.

–Nadia Mathews

Made in the USA
Charleston, SC
25 January 2011